Poker Tournament Strategies

By
Sylvester Suzuki

A product of Two Plus Two Publishing
www.twoplustwo.com

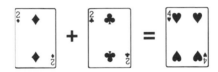

SECOND EDITION

FIRST PRINTING
June 2004

Printing and Binding
Creel Printing Co.
Las Vegas, Nevada

Printed in the United States of America

Poker Tournament Strategies
COPYRIGHT © 1998 TWO PLUS TWO PUBLISHING

For information contact:
Two Plus Two Publishing
600 West Sunset
Suite 103
Henderson NV 89015
(702) 896-1326

ISBN: 1-880685-19-1

To those dedicated men and women who serve as dealers in poker tournaments all across this great land. With your patience and perseverance, you make it all happen.   Many thanks.

Table of Contents

Foreword
by Mason Malmuth

Poker tournaments have hit the big time, and when I say big time I don't just mean the great events like the World Series of Poker held every spring at Binion's Horseshoe Hotel and Casino in Las Vegas and the televised tournaments from the World Poker Tour. I mean all poker tournaments including those with very small buy-ins.

Oddly enough, though, many of the best tournament players don't do well in standard ring games, and many of the top side-game players perform poorly in tournaments. There is a very good reason for this: Ring games and tournaments are very different.

In a side game, whether it be stud, hold 'em, or another form of poker, you are generally trying to weave a "web of deception" that will allow you to maximize your results on every hand you play. In a tournament, depending on your situation, you will either be trying to accumulate chips, be on the attack, or trying to survive. In many situations this will lead to dramatic changes in strategy from what would normally be correct.

Tournaments can also be very exciting. One particularly dramatic example of this occurred in the $10,000 no-limit championship event at the 1982 World Series of Poker. Jack Straus was down to one chip. After managing to bluff off most of his assets, he played survival poker and made an incredible comeback to be proclaimed World Champion. He also gave credence to the saying that all you need is a "chip and a chair."

Author Sylvester Suzuki has played a lot of tournaments. While Suzuki is a pen name, he is a real person who not only has much experience to draw conclusions from, but who understands the underlying theory that governs tournament play. What follows is a very dynamic book. It should prove helpful to virtually everyone interested in tournament play and is an excellent guide for those of you who are new to this form of poker. I recommend that you read it more than once and, of course, get some experience playing "the tourneys."

About Sylvester Suzuki

Sylvester Suzuki is the pen name of a freelance writer who currently resides in southern California. As a teenager in the late 1940s, Mr. Suzuki, who was born and raised in the Seattle area, began his poker-playing career with such penny-ante favorites as "baseball" and "spit in the ocean." He then steadily progressed to no-limit lowball as a merchant seaman in the mid-fifties.

Shortly after graduating from the University of Washington in 1959, Suzuki departed for assignment as a civilian administrative officer with the Eight United States Army in Seoul, Korea. During a twenty-five-year career with several Department of Defense agencies, primarily in overseas areas, Suzuki was a poker-playing regular in a variety of officers clubs, bachelor officers quarters, and on-base family housing facilities.

Since his retirement in 1984, Mr. Suzuki has been playing poker primarily in the casinos of California and Nevada.

A Note on the Text

This text addresses several different kinds of poker tournaments, and they *are* very different. Consequently it was decided to write this book in sections with the first five sections each addressing a different form of poker. This way, if you want a quick review of a particular type, you will only need to read (or reread) the appropriate section instead of the whole book.

However, even tournaments that appear and are very different, can and do have many aspects that are similar. For instance, the final table at a Progressive Stack Rebuy Tournament is very similar to the final table at a No Rebuy Tournament even though the early rounds are certainly not the same.

Because of this, and the fact that this text was put together in sections, some of the material or something very similar appears in more than one place, and some readers of the first edition found this annoying. However, both the author and the publisher feel that even though this is the case, the way the book is structured is the best way. This should benefit those of you who are interested in more than one quick reading.

Note: For those of you interested in taking your tournament game to the highest level, we recommend *Tournament Poker for Advanced Players* by David Sklansky.

Introduction

Winning at the poker table in a card casino is not easy. Not only are players in casinos very competitive, but the casino must also take its share, and over time, this house "rake" can add up to a substantial amount. If you stop and think about it, it could not possibly be otherwise. It costs a tremendous amount of money to operate a casino and obviously, someone has to pay for the rent, utilities, salaries, and so forth. In the long run, that someone will have to be you and me, the patrons of the casino.

In this respect, the situation in a casino is very different from the typical neighborhood home game. Except for a small amount of money that is collected to pay for the beer and snacks, for every dollar that is lost by a player in a home game, a dollar is won by another. The win-loss balance is different in a casino, and even the winner contributes a share to maintain the game. Although the higher caliber of play in the casinos is undoubtedly a contributing factor, the large drain on funds has its impact on all players. This includes those who win in neighborhood home games, but who fail to adjust to the more competitive casino environment.

Still, there are a small number of players who are highly successful in the commercial cardrooms. Some of these players "graduate" to the middle- and high-limit games, and some go on to become tournament experts.

How do you reach this level of success? A few do it very quickly because they are extremely talented. Most others who succeed do so because they have access to good information and work hard at improving their poker skills.

So what about you, the average poker player? How likely are you to succeed at casino poker and perhaps attain the status of a professional? The answer to this question depends largely upon how willing you are to work at improving your game.

In other words, if you are endowed with only modest poker-playing ability, you are not destined to be a perpetual loser in the casinos. By working on your game, and picking your situations carefully and wisely, it is possible to be an overall winner without having truly "world-class" ability. In all honesty, I can make no promises of fame and riches, but I can promise you the realistic prospect of becoming an overall winner at the small buy-in poker tournaments if you carefully read, assimilate, and apply the information contained in the pages of this book.

Before proceeding further, it's a good idea to familiarize yourself with the definitions in the glossary. A thorough knowledgw of these terms will greatly facilitate reading and understanding what follows.

One more point. The object of this book is not to provide you with information on poker-playing strategy. Rather, with the assumption that you are already a competent player, this book is written to provide basic poker *tournament* strategy. Its main target are the small stakes in-house tournaments that are being conducted on a daily basis in casinos across the country, but we will also touch upon the larger tournaments that attract some of the best tournament players in the world. Also, to help clarify some of the information in the text we will occasionally get involved with "poker game" strategy as opposed to "poker tournament" strategy. This is done for your benefit.

If you feel that your general poker knowledge needs improvement, see Appendix B in the back of this book for some recommended reading. If you are just getting started, I recommend that you start with the small in-house tournaments that have buy-ins ranging from $10 to $30.

By the way, we shall see that tournament poker is sometimes very different from play in a "ring game." A play that would be routine at an open table can sometimes lead to disaster in a poker tournament. One of the objects of this book, therefore, is to point out some of these situations and hopefully help you on the road to success.

Finally, we would like to express our appreciation to Paula Cizmar for editing this work. Thanks to her, our ideas are now more clearly stated and thus, should be more easily understood. In addition, we wish to thank Dave Clint for his cover design and art work throughout this book, and Donna Harris for her comments and proof reading.

Background

As this is being written, the major casinos in Los Angeles County sponsor more than thirty-five regular weekly poker tournaments with buy-ins of less than $30 and service charges of $5 or less. A review of *Card Player Magazine* indicates that these small-stakes tournaments are becoming increasingly popular across the country. Obviously, with such a small amount being deducted by the casinos, these tournaments offer the small stakes player an opportunity to compete successfully in the casino environment. Before you begin, however, it would be wise to learn about some of the nuances of tournament play.

In addition to these small-stakes in-house tournaments, many of the large casinos sponsor major tournaments that have buy-ins ranging from as low as $120 to as high as $10,000 for the main event of the World Series of Poker at Binion's Horseshoe Hotel and Casino in Las Vegas and $25,000 for the final event of the World Poker Tour.

One of the key differences between playing in a tournament and playing at an open table on the casino floor is that you cannot cash in at your convenience. As a result, at various points in a tournament, preserving a portion of your stack (in essence, surviving) may be a more important consideration than maximizing the amount you can win with a particular hand.

This is very different from open table play where generally your objective is to maximize your winnings on each hand you play. As an example, assume you are in the last position in a seven-card stud tournament with only eight players remaining. The eighth place finisher will receive $20, the seventh place finisher will receive $30, and the sixth place finisher will receive $50. Further assume that a player bets $1,000 in tournament chips after the last card has been dealt and you have $1,100 in tournament chips remaining and a hand that is nearly certain to

7

win. Would it be wise to raise with your last $100? In a ring game, you would put every penny you have into the pot. But in a tournament, that may not be the best move. In fact, in a tournament your move would depend on how management determines tournament placings when two or more players are eliminated from the tournament during the course of a hand. This is explained in Part Seven of this book.

Another important characteristic of tournament play was first pointed out by Mason Malmuth in his book *Gambling Theory and Other Topics:* In almost all tournaments, the average value of each chip will change as play progresses. This is very different from play at an open table on the casino floor where the value of a chip is always equal to the amount shown on the chip. A chip at an open table that indicates a value of $10 is always worth $10. In a tournament, the value of a chip that indicates a value of $10 could be worth far more than $10 or only a fraction of $10, depending on a host of factors.

How is this possible? The value of a chip changes during the course of a tournament because:

1.   The winner of a tournament normally receives only a fraction of the money that is in the tournament pool. For example, assume that there is $2,000 in the tournament pool and that the winner of the tournament will receive $1,000 and the second place finisher will receive $500. If no additional chips were sold during the tournament, by the end of the tournament, the average value of each chip will have declined to only 25 percent of the original value (from a percentage of $2,000 to the same percentage of $500). The reason is that when the last two players begin play, they are actually only playing for the $500 difference between first place and second place.

2.   The relative value of each chip in the tournament will vary. Let's look at a simple example. Suppose you are not only

fortunate enough to enter the $10,000 no-limit championship at the World Series of Poker, but you win it as well and collect the million dollars. What impact does this have on your chips?

Well, to start with, for your $10,000 entry fee you get $10,000 in tournament chips. So when play begins your chips were worth their face value. But when the tournament is finished, assuming that there are approximately one thousand entries, you should have approximately $10 million in tournament chips, which you then exchange for perhaps $3 million. It's a pretty good prize, but it seems as if your chips lost 70 percent of their value.

In reality, depending on how many people are left, your chips may have lost even more value than this. For instance, the second place finisher in the World Championship usually gets about half of what the first place finisher gets. This means that once it gets down to two players, you will be playing for only the difference between first and second place. From this point of view the chips have now lost approximately 85 percent of their value.

The above example is only one illustration of the fact that in a poker tournament that pays only a percentage of the money in the tournament pool to the winner, the average value of a chip in a small stack is higher than the average value of a chip in a large stack. The exception to this is when only two players are remaining. Now all chips are worth their proportion of the difference between first and second place.

Hence, the adage that when a player goes broke in a percentage payback tournament, it is correct strategy to make a rebuy. (In practice however, there may be factors that mitigate against making a rebuy such as the position of the blinds, the size of the rebuy stack, the size of the other stacks at your table, the skill of the other players at your table, and so forth.)

To summarize, you need to know that *the fewer chips you have the more each chip is worth, and the more chips you have the less each chip is worth.* In addition, this effect becomes stronger as the tournament progresses.

3. Additional chips are frequently sold at a reduced price as play progresses. For example, at one of the casinos in Los Angeles County, for the buy-in of $13 (including the $3 service charge), players receive $200 in tournament chips. However, after the first twenty minutes of play, players receive $300 in tournament chips for each $10 rebuy, and $400 in tournament chips after the first forty minutes of play for each $10 rebuy. As a result, after the first twenty minutes of play, the number of chips in the tournament is increasing faster than the number of dollars in the tournament pool. Therefore, after the first twenty minutes of play, the average value of each chip declines until no more rebuys are permitted.

Prior to commencing work on this book, we conducted a survey of various casinos across the country. The survey revealed that:

1. The most popular buy-in for regularly scheduled in-house tournaments is in the range of $13 to $25. There are also a few free entry tournaments. However, almost all free tournaments sell additional chips during the course of the tournament. In such cases, for purposes of the recommendations contained here, the cost of the first rebuy should be considered to be equivalent to the buy-in.

2. The overwhelming majority of casinos use the percentage payback method of paying tournament finalists.

3. The vast majority of small tournaments offered by casinos are multiple rebuy tournaments that offer rebuys for one hour.

4.   Variations in other tournament procedures are virtually endless. Since it is impossible to discuss in detail every type of tournament that is being offered, this book will concentrate primarily on the most common types of percentage payback tournaments. These are:

A.   Multiple rebuy tournaments in which rebuy stacks increase in size without an increase in cost as the tournament progresses. These tournaments, known as "Progressive Stack Rebuy Tournaments," are discussed in Part One of this book.

B.   Tournaments that do not permit rebuys. These "No Rebuy Tournaments" are discussed in Part Two of this book.

C.   Multiple rebuy tournaments in which the size of the rebuy stack does not increase. These tournaments, known as "Constant Stack Rebuy Tournaments" are discussed in Part Three of this book.

Although relatively rare in our casinos today "Shootout Tournaments" and "Sudden Sayonara Tournaments" are also discussed in their own sections because of the vast differences in playing strategy that these two types of tournaments require. (See Parts Four and Five of this book respectively.)

Satellite tournaments are not really tournaments in themselves, but merely adjuncts of major tournaments. Also, because satellite tournaments are almost as varied as the small stakes tournaments discussed in this book, our commentary on satellite tournaments will be limited to a few brief remarks.

I am not an advocate of satellite tournaments. For one thing, I believe that service charges for most satellite tournaments are excessive when compared to most small-stakes in-house tournaments where an equal or greater amount can be won.

12 Background

Further, I personally find that regular in-house tournaments are a more promising source of funds for entering one of the larger tournaments. The fact that the caliber of play in most satellites seems to be a bit higher than regular in-house tournaments is also a factor affecting my preference for the in-house tournament.

The majority of satellite tournaments operate on the one-table winner-take-all principle, with the winner gaining access to a larger tournament. In essence, a one-table satellite is virtually identical to the first table of a shootout tournament. Even though there is much skill involved in the playing of a one-table satellite, this is only the case if the time allotted to it is of a reasonable length. Occasionally I've seen a one-table satellite beginning less than thirty minutes before the start of the main tournament. To complete the satellite on a timely basis, limits were raised at five-minute intervals. Why do tournament managers insist on wasting time in this manner? If they're really serious about speeding up the process and eliminating the skill factor, why not just have the entrants to the satellite draw cards to determine the winner?

Most of the satellite tournaments that are not one-table satellites are basically multiple rebuy Constant Stack Rebuy Tournaments with the winners gaining entry to the larger tournament. However, depending on the size of the tournament pool, more than one player may gain entry to the larger tournament, and one or more players who do not gain entry to the larger tournament may receive a portion of the prize money. For example, if the buy-in for the larger tournament is $550 and the tournament pool is $1,400, it is normal procedure to award two entries to the larger tournament. Usually, the $300 remaining would be awarded to the third place finisher. However, a different distribution might be made.

Before you enter any tournament, be it a small-stakes tournament, a satellite tournament, or a major tournament, be certain that you understand the rules, especially the payout procedures, beforehand. Keep in mind that if more than one player will gain entry to the larger tournament, the objective is not to win the satellite but to get a main tournament seat. In other words, your objective is not to win, but to survive, survive, survive. As you will see throughout the course of this book, however, surviving is *not* the same as just "playing tight."

Many examples will be presented here of ill-considered decisions that some small tournament regulars make with barely a thought because the buy-ins and rebuys are cheap. (I'm sure that many similar mistakes are made by some players in the larger tournaments.) Don't fall into this trap yourself. If you really do want to be a winning player in the casinos, you must learn to be disciplined. Over the course of months and years, those routine decisions that you and your competitors make will inevitably separate the winners from the losers. While it is true that short term luck often determines who will win the tournament on any given day, in the long run, it will invariably be the skilled and the disciplined players who will be successful. There may be some exceptions, but prudence dictates that you not count on this being the case.

Part One

Progressive Stack
Rebuy Tournaments

Progressive Stack Rebuy Tournaments

Introduction

For years many tournament players had a complaint. They felt that rebuys weren't worth making after the betting limits had been raised a couple times since the amount of chips they were receiving was now equivalent to only a small number of bets. As we will see later in this book, this logic is flawed. In an effort to satisfy these complaints however, Progressive Stack Rebuy Tournaments were born — and in many locations they have become very popular.

For those of you unfamiliar with Progressive Stack Rebuy Tournaments, these are simply events that allow rebuys and for which you get more in tournament chips the later in the rebuy period it is. This solved the late-in-the-game rebuy complaint, allowing players to feel that when they make a rebuy they would get enough chips (and bets) so that they could still compete.

Overview

Progressive stack rebuy tournaments that pay finalists a percentage of the tournament pool are the most common type of small poker tournaments currently being conducted in casinos across the United States. An example of current tournaments of this type in one casino is as follows:

1. Number of tournaments each week: 12

2. Buy-in: $13 (including $3 service charge) for $200 in tournament chips

3. Rebuys:

   a. First 20 minutes: $10 for $200 in tournament chips. Must have less than $200 in tournament chips to qualify for the rebuy.

   b. Second 20 minutes: $10 for $300 in tournament chips. Must have less than $300 in tournament chips to qualify for the rebuy.

   c. Third 20 minutes: $10 for $400 in tournament chips. Must have less than $400 in tournament chips to qualify for the rebuy.

4. Add-on: One $10 add-on for $400 in tournament chips is permitted after a 10 minute intermission regardless of the number of chips in a player's stack at the end of the first 60 minutes of play. Players with less than $400 in chips may make a simultaneous rebuy and add-on ($800 in tournament chips for $20).

17

5.   Betting limits:

Betting Limits	
20 minutes	$10-$20
20 minutes	$15-$30
20 minutes	$30-$60
Intermission	
20 minutes	$50-$100
20 minutes	$100-$200
20 minutes	$150-$300
Intermission	
20 minutes	$200-$400
20 minutes	$300-$600
20 minutes	$500-$1,000

Limits are raised at 20-minute intervals until the conclusion of the tournament.

6.   Number of players: 65-140

7.   Tournament pool: $1,200-$3,500

8.   Tournament payout (an actual example of a typical day)

Tournament Payouts			
Place	Payout	Place	Payout
1	$800	10	$20
2	$520	11	$20
3	$270	12	$10
4	$155	13	$10
5	$135	14	$10
6	$110	15	$10
7	$90	16	$10
8	$70	17	$10
9	$55	18	$10

One characteristic of these progressive stack rebuy tournaments is that in the early stages of the tournament, the action is almost always very loose. However, after the end of the rebuy period, the pace changes abruptly. The reason is that when players know they can rebuy for only a few dollars, they will be inclined to play a lot of hands.

Another important characteristic of these tournaments is that when play commences after the end of the rebuy period, almost all the players will have stacks of approximately equal size. (No-limit tournaments are an exception and will be addressed separately.) Why do almost all players start with equal size stacks after the intermission? Because it only costs $10 to rebuy and the progressive nature of the rebuy stack encourages players to rebuy and add-on.

Does this mean that how you play during the rebuy period is not really very important? Not at all. *It is very important.* And, over a period of many tournaments, it will make a difference. Players who play well during the early stages of these progressive stack tournaments will have a significant, indeed crucial, advantage over rivals who play loosely because it is still cheap to rebuy.

Any player who has increased his stack sixfold, usually from $200 to $1,200 in tournament chips, in the first sixty minutes of play without a rebuy has done extremely well. He can then add-on an additional amount, usually $400 in tournament chips for the rebuy, at a typical cost of $10. Does this mean that the $1,200 in tournament chips that he has at the end of the first sixty minutes of play is worth only $30, or $20 more than he paid for his original stack of $200 (in tournament chips)? (Ignore the service charge; that money is gone.)

Contrary to the opinion of many tournament regulars, it does not. The reason is that in this example the chips in the tournament at the end of the rebuy period were purchased at rates of $200, $300, and $400 per $10. Therefore, the actual value of the $1,200 in tournament chips can be determined only after all rebuys and add-ons have been made. This amount can then be approximated by taking the $1,200 as a percentage of the total number of chips in the tournament and multiplying that percentage by the total amount of money in the tournament pool. The reason why it is only an approximation is that since all stacks are not of equal size, as was pointed out earlier, the value of each chip is not exactly equal. However, at this stage of the tournament, the impact of this effect is still fairly minimal.

Therefore, if there is a total of $2,000 in the tournament pool and $60,000 in tournament chips, the approximate value of the $1,200 in tournament chips would be around $40:

$$\$40 \ = \ (\$2,000)\left(\frac{1,200 \ chips}{60,000 \ chips} \right)$$

There's a good reason why this is being addressed: Many small tournament players, including many of the regulars, seem to underestimate the value of their chips in the early stages of a tournament. This also leads to extremely loose play and an excessive number of rebuys. In the long run, among players of relatively equal ability, how a player plays in the early stages of these small-stakes tournaments will inevitably separate the winners from the losers. The reason is not only because players who avoid making early rebuys are not investing as much money into each tournament, but also because these players are buying chips more cheaply than the player who routinely makes those early rebuys. This idea is extremely important and cannot be over emphasized because, as we shall see, it has an important impact on overall playing strategy for Progressive Stack Rebuy Tournaments.

The First Twenty Minutes

Play is usually extremely loose during the rebuy period as mentioned earlier. But: Do not fall into this trap, especially during the first twenty minutes of play. Why? Very simply, if you have to rebuy, you will typically only receive $200 in chips. If, in the first few minutes of play, you find that you are in danger of being forced to make a rebuy, play solid, conservative poker. If, however, you have a larger stack than your adversary, be aggressive and try to force him to make a rebuy while the rebuy stack is still at this level. If successful, notice that you will be making him invest more to acquire the same number of chips as most other players when the rebuy period has ended. In addition, you will have to invest less to accomplish the same purpose.

Some writers on poker tournament strategy advocate playing fast in the early stages of a rebuy tournament (if you intend to rebuy) because it will give you a chance to build a large stack prior to the end of the rebuy period. This advice may be appropriate for a Constant Stack Rebuy Tournament, but in the long run it is clearly not appropriate for a Progressive Stack Rebuy Tournament. If playing fast is likely to put you in a position where you might be forced to make an early rebuy while tournament chips are still being sold at a premium price, you need to slow down.

To avoid being forced to make an early rebuy, many tournament players do not take their seat until well after the tournament has started. Although this strategy is probably superior to the strategy (or lack thereof) of players who come out swinging on the first hand that has been dealt, it is also deficient because:

1.   They are giving away antes or blinds;

2. With many empty seats at the table, they are missing opportunities to steal antes and/or blinds from other absent players;

3. They are missing an opportunity to observe the other players at their table and identify patterns and tendencies in some of their opponents.

Quite often, when the tournament starts, there will be only three or four players at the table. Besides the attempt to avoid an early rebuy, another reason many small tournament regulars come late to the table is that they believe that since the initial blinds are small, the first few minutes of play are not important. They are wrong! These absent players are giving their seated opponents who will steal their antes and blinds a chip lead. Even though that chip lead may be rather small, it can be very important in the early stages of a tournament. That's because without going all-in themselves, players with a chip lead will be in a position to force players with smaller stacks to go all-in while the rebuy stack is still at its minimum — usually $200 in tournament chips.

Obviously, this advantage is more significant in a no-limit tournament because a player will often go all-in with his first raise. But even in a limit game do not underestimate the advantage of a small chip lead in the early minutes of a tournament. It will often determine who will be making the early rebuys — and in the long run, the players who are making the early rebuys will be the losers. This will be true even though they may have their share of placings in the money because they will, in general, be paying more to get there.

Another common error that some players make in the early stages of tournament play warrants your attention. Assume that you have only $5 in chips and have the dealer button in a hold 'em

tournament with

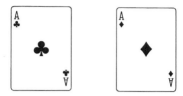

The blinds are $5 and $10, and the rebuy stack will increase to $300 (from $200) in the next few minutes. Would it be proper strategy to play this hand against the two blinds? Even though you are holding the best possible starting hand, the answer is that you should quickly muck it because the most that you will be able to win with the hand is only $10, and the pair of aces is far from a certainty to win. By waiting for the rebuy stack to increase, you will be certain to get an additional $100. When playing in a Progressive Stack Rebuy Tournament, always watch the clock and play accordingly. Try to avoid paying a premium for chips that will be discounted soon thereafter. This is just one example of how tournament play can differ from correct strategy in a standard ring game.

Since betting limits at the start are typically only $10 and $20, players who are playing these tournaments well should seldom find themselves being forced to make a rebuy during the first twenty minutes. The exception is when the tournament is no-limit.

Even with blinds of only $5 and $10, it is possible to quickly accumulate a large stack in a no-limit tournament because many players will not hesitate to make an all-in call with a mediocre starting hand. They are aware that many others are also playing loosely and it will only cost a small amount to make a rebuy. Again, don't fall into this trap yourself. Be prepared to play very aggressively when appropriate, especially if you have a larger stack than your adversary and/or believe that you have the best of it going in. Remember you want to force them to make an early rebuy while not doing so yourself.

Use this situation for what it is: an excellent opportunity to build your stack and start play after the intermission with a huge chip lead because none of your competitors will be able to buy more than two add-ons (typically $800) in tournament chips during the intermission. At a loose table, with a run of good fortune, it is sometimes possible to accumulate a stack of $4,000 to $5,000 in tournament chips without making a single rebuy. While it is certainly true that a tournament cannot be won in the early stages of play, in a no-limit tournament you can go a long way toward attaining that goal. Don't miss this opportunity. Of course, it won't happen every time you play, but it will come along often enough that you should always be ready to take advantage of it. So be aggressive with your good hands, especially against someone who will call your big bets with mediocre hands.

The Second Twenty Minutes

Recommended playing strategy for the second twenty minutes of play is essentially the same as the first twenty minutes. However, since the rebuy stack has increased, usually from $200 to $300, players who are playing on short stacks may wish to liberalize their conservative stance a bit.

Of course, this is counterbalanced to some degree by the fact that some players who have started poorly begin to play recklessly in an effort to catch up. Needless to say, not only will their rebuys add to the tournament pool, but their loose play will sometimes present opportunities that you can use to your advantage.

For example, in a hold 'em tournament small pairs from any position can be profitable if you know that loose players are present at your table. Now if you flop a set you will be assured of plenty of action. But again, keep in mind the idea that you want your opponents to rebuy while you do not want to make this purchase. So while a small pair may become playable because you either flop a set or fold, a hand like a small suited connector would not because it can be very expensive on both the flop and turn to attempt to make your flush or straight.

The Third Twenty Minutes

Since the rebuy stack has been stabilized — typically at $400 in tournament chips — in tournaments where there are betting limits, there is little need to consider special tournament strategy as opposed to poker strategy. (One exception is discussed below.) In other words, play each hand according to the value of that hand.

If you are eligible to make a rebuy at this point, ignoring for the moment such factors as the position of the dealer button, the strength of the players at your table, and so forth, it is always correct strategy to do so. By making a rebuy in the third thirty minutes you will be causing the average value of each chip in the tournament to decline. This means that when you make a rebuy, the value of every other player's stack will drop. Obviously, this is to your benefit. So, if you find yourself eligible to make a rebuy during this period of time, do so immediately. For example, if you have $395 in tournament chips, purchase some more of them. Otherwise, you may lose your eligibility to make a rebuy by winning the next hand.

This brings us to a related point. If you play one of these tournaments and don't intend to rebuy at all you will be putting yourself at a disadvantage to those players who rebuy correctly. In fact, proper rebuy strategy is almost as important as how you play your hands.

The flip side to this is that if it is advantageous for you to rebuy, it is also detrimental for you when other players rebuy. There is therefore less incentive for you to put other players all-in unless you feel there is a good chance that the player in question will "go home." (This would be the one exception to not considering any special tournament strategy at this stage in the tournament.)

Now this does not mean to suggest that you should withdraw into a conservative shell for the next twenty minutes. Play each hand according to its intrinsic value — which in poker frequently suggests aggressive play. Even though rebuy theory is very important, it is still early in the tournament and you would like to add to your chip position.

In the last minutes before the intermission, some players will be playing very loosely in order to play down their stack to below the rebuy threshold. That will qualify them to make an additional rebuy. Is this good tournament strategy? That depends on several factors such as:

1. How far will the player have to play down his stack?
2. What is the strength of the player's hand?
3. How likely is the player to be raised?

Since betting limits during this period are typically $30 and $60, it may be possible to play down your stack for as little as $15 (from the small blind). That clearly would be worth doing. However, the complexity and multiplicity of factors that need to be considered in playing down your stack renders it impractical to attempt to formulate any exact standards. My personal rule of thumb for these tournaments is: approximately $60 or one big bet.[1] If I do not feel that I have a reasonable chance to win the pot, I will not play down my stack for more than this. If there is no legitimate chance for me to win the pot, I am practically giving another player some of my chips, and these are chips that I had to pay for and he did not.

In a no-limit tournament, as the end of the rebuy period approaches, you will find that there are large differences in the size of stacks at your table. This happens because many all-in hands have been played and the rebuy stack is relatively small when compared to the chip holdings of the players who had been successful in the tournament up to that time. At this stage, because

---

[1] Assuming again that losing this "$60" allows you to purchase another "$400" in tournament chips for $10.

unlimited rebuys are permitted, there is a tendency for some players to play what is known as desperation poker in the hope of building a large stack before the rebuy period ends. In other words, these players are calling and raising with hands that, on their own merit, do not justify such action.

Note that during this time frame, the blinds are still relatively small. Therefore, a sizable pot can be won only if the blinds are raised. If you have a short stack and cards that do not really justify such action, would it be correct to bring it in for a raise? Probably not. You have little to gain unless you get a call, and if called (or raised), you will probably be up against a superior hand. Rather than playing an inferior hand in such an aggressive manner — and most likely helping some other player build a stack — I recommend a more conservative approach. Continue to play solid, sensible poker and make an add-on at the intermission. Keep in mind that although the big stacks will have a decided advantage after the intermission, in poker, especially no-limit poker, the pendulum sometimes swings very quickly. In other words, always remember that poker is a game of patience. While it is true that the stakes will be increasing rapidly, you still have time to let your poker skills play their part.

Special Note

What I have been discussing is a series of actual small stakes rebuy tournaments. As mentioned earlier, these types of tournaments are the most common small-stakes tournaments in our casinos. However, the variations are almost endless and one of these is appropriate for discussion while we are on the subject of rebuys.

I have played in some tournaments (although fortunately not recently) in which the add-on stack was as much as double the last rebuy stack. In other words, if applied to the preceding model, the add-on stack would be $800 in tournament chips for only $10. In my opinion, this makes absolutely no sense because with such a structure it would probably be proper strategy to play virtually no hands during the rebuy period — except when it is possible to steal antes or blinds from absent players. By not playing any hands except the certain steals, it is possible to survive the rebuy period with the original stack and make an add-on. This will allow you to start the second session of play with a minimum investment and a reasonably competitive stack. But think about it: What fun would that be? Having played in over a thousand small-stakes poker tournaments over the years, I am convinced that the vast majority of small stakes tournament players are recreational players who are there for the fun of it. Even so, I'm sure we'll all agree: Winning is invariably more fun than losing.

The Intermediate Stage

The intermediate stage of the tournament is defined as that period of time extending from the end of the rebuy period to the part when players begin to look toward other tables in order to count the number of heads remaining in the tournament. This usually begins when the number of players remaining is approximately one full table more than the number who will finish in the money. For the purpose of our model, therefore, the intermediate stage ends when there are approximately twenty-seven players remaining. Usually, this will occur seventy-five to ninety minutes after rebuys have ended.

As we pointed out, immediately after the intermission the pace of the action usually slows. This change is so apparent that no experienced tournament player could fail to notice it. It occurs because the players have just lost their psychological safety net, the rebuy option. Plus, when there are no more rebuys, the incentive to play fast has declined, and survival has become a more important consideration.

What are the implications for the astute tournament player? You should take advantage of this tight play by being more aggressive yourself, particularly if you are up against a shorter stack or you are the first one excluding the blinds to enter the pot. Otherwise, play solid, patient poker through the rest of this period. Actually, what is known as "attrition poker" will be played — it's attrition poker because no more rebuys are permitted, and when a player loses what chips he has, he is eliminated from the tournament.

The End Game

The end game is defined as the period from the end of the intermediate stage to the conclusion of the tournament. It is also that time where many tournament skills come into play.

The tournament payout shown in the first paragraph of this chapter was based on actual figures for a tournament. Note that the tenth through the eighteenth finishers were paid only a total of $110. It is therefore probable that all of them actually lost money playing in the tournament. Why do tournament managers bother to pay players as little as $10? Because they are, for the most part, shrewd promoters. They realize that for purely psychological reasons, many players get a feeling of satisfaction in having won something when they finish in the money, even if they actually lost money in the tournament. This is commonly done in other casino tournaments as well. For example, in Nevada, many slot tournaments pay something to half of the participants. These small amounts that are paid to the players will of course have an impact on how they will play in the last few minutes of the tournament.

As the number of players remaining declines to near the payoff point, you will notice that most of the players who have small stacks will begin to play very conservatively because they want to finish in the money. Is this good tournament strategy?

With the actual payout structure mentioned, it definitely is not because the payoffs are so small for just getting into the money. If you find yourself at this stage of a tournament with a small stack, my recommendation is that you do the opposite. Aggressively take advantage of the tight play of your opponents and try to position yourself for a real payday. That is, when the opportunity presents itself, be willing to attack these other short stacks. However, if one of these conservative players comes in with a raise, that's an indication they have a quality hand and many hands that you would normally play in a regular game should now be folded.

Of course, I want to caution you that the tournament payout structure described above is by no means universal. Most tournaments of this size and type will pay only players who survive to the last table. Since a payout of $60-$70 for a small tournament such as this is much better than a $10 payoff, finishing in the money becomes more meaningful. Therefore, playing survival poker becomes more attractive. However, taking advantage of tight play may still be a profitable alternative that you should keep in mind.

Proper strategy in the end game is chip dependent. That is, the size of your stack should dictate your approach. Here's how you should handle strategy depending on your chip position.

1. **You have one of the large stacks.** Concentrate on eliminating players who have small stacks. If another player with a large stack bets into you, do not get into a raising war with him until you are virtually certain that you have the winning hand. Keep in mind that with a large stack, you should be able to at least finish in the money. Another player with a large stack might be able to eliminate you from the tournament with one big hand. A player with a short stack cannot.

    Let's elaborate on this point a little more. Suppose I have a large stack and instead of having a virtual cinch, I just think that I have "way the best of it." Here's exactly how to play.

    A. I will bet into another large stack, but if he raises would only call.

    B. If he bets into me, I will merely call. Only very rarely would I consider raising.

Put another way, I will not get into a raising war with another large stack unless I have a "virtual" cinch.

So why is this the case? In a standard ring game it would certainly be correct to be much more aggressive. But we must understand that at this stage of the tournament — the end game — tournament play frequently differs dramatically from standard ring game play. Because of the percentage payback nature of tournaments, when two large stacks clash, especially late in an event, all other remaining players will benefit regardless of which player wins the pot.

To see exactly how this works, let's look at the following example. Let's say there are only three players left in a tournament that pays 60 percent for first place, 30 percent for second place, and 10 percent for third place, and each player has exactly $1,000 in front of him. With $3,000 in the tournament this means that first place is worth $1,800, second is worth $900, and the third finisher receives $300.

$$1,800 = (.60)(3,000)$$

$$900 = (.30)(3,000)$$

$$300 = (.10)(3,000)$$

However, if they are all equal players, then each player at this point should expect to win an average of $1,000.

$$1,000 = \left(\frac{1}{3}\right)(1,800) + \left(\frac{1}{3}\right)(900) + \left(\frac{1}{3}\right)(300)$$

Suppose at this point that players A and B get all-in against each other while player C sits out. Suppose also that before the last card it is determined that it is exactly fifty-fifty as far as which of the two hands will win.

Let us now determine player A's expectation for the tournament. One-half of the time he will lose the pot and thus get the $300 third prize. The other half of the time he will win the pot and thus be a 2-to-1 favorite (since he now has $2,000) to beat player C heads-up. He will therefore come in third one-half of the time, second one-sixth of the time, and first one-third of the time.

His expectation is now $900.

$$900 = \left(\frac{1}{2}\right)(300) + \left(\frac{1}{6}\right)(900) + \left(\frac{1}{3}\right)(1,800)$$

The same calculation would hold true for player B. But how can this be? Both players A and B started their hand with an expectation of $1,000. They are now gambling on a dead-even proposition. Yet somehow this even gamble seems to be costing both of them money in the long run.

Where has this extra $200 gone? Has player C somehow gotten it just by sitting out the pot? Well, let's figure it out.

Regardless of the outcome of the contest between A and B, player C will find himself a 2-to-1 underdog to the winner. His expectation is therefore

$$\left(\frac{1}{3}\right)(1,800) + \left(\frac{2}{3}\right)(900)$$

This comes out to $1,200. He does indeed pick up $200 "equity" by just watching.[2]

---

[2]This example was originally presented in the book *Sklansky on Poker* by David Sklansky; it appears here with the

Consequently, there is value in minimizing the degree of the clash. Thus, I recommend not to get into a raising war very late in a tournament unless you have a virtual cinch.

There is of course, another reason why you as a player with a large stack should prefer to go up against a player with a small stack. As was mentioned earlier, his chips are actually more valuable than yours. Of course, if you win his chips they are not worth more in your stack. However, the penalty to him for losing the hand is far greater than the penalty to you for having a negative result.

2. **You have a medium size stack.** You are probably not in immediate danger of elimination. Try to avoid confrontations with players who have larger stacks unless you feel you have a clear advantage, and concentrate on the smaller stacks. If you do decide to commit yourself to a promising hand, do so decisively and aggressively with the attitude that you are going to position yourself to win the tournament with this hand. Good poker often dictates that you act decisively because aggressive action on your part can cause your opponents to make errors and help tip the scales in your favor. However, if the hand appears to go sour and you can save a few chips, you should always do so. As long as you still have a chip, you have a chance.

Here are two examples of this last idea. In a hold 'em tournament if you start with

permission of David Sklansky.

and the flop comes

be ready to give it up. Similarly when playing stud if you start with

and catch the

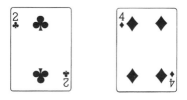

on fourth and fifth streets respectively, and your opponent has a reasonable board, again be ready to give it up. In both of these examples you are usually better off saving any chips you can.

3. **You have one of the small stacks.** You will not have the luxury of waiting for a premium hand. In games that are played with blinds, the position of the dealer button is often far more important than the skill of the players. Pay close attention to the location of the dealer button and the stacks of

players who will be required to post blinds before you do. If players who will be required to post blinds before you have small stacks, consider the possibility that you might be able to avoid posting because of the movement of players and/or the consolidation of tables. If you do decide that you must commit yourself to a hand, do so aggressively. However, always bear in mind that if you can save even one chip, that might be enough to move you up the payout ladder.

Finally, to finish this section there are two ideas related to blind play that I wish to mention.

1. For games that are played with blinds, be aware that players with small stacks will often be forced to commit to less than ideal starting hands because of the size of the blinds. Be prepared to stand your ground if you have a reasonable number of chips against players with small stacks who come on aggressively, especially if that player is in a position where he will soon be required to put up the big blind. (This concept is particularly true if you can easily put them all-in.)

    By the same logic, if you see a player with a small stack bring it in for a raise and he has several hands to go before he is required to put up a blind, give him credit for a good hand. In my experience, even in the smallest tournaments, few players play poorly enough to come out charging from a favorable position with a weak hand.

2. If you are in a late position, particularly if you are in the dealer position, the chip status of the two blinds becomes increasingly important because almost all players with small stacks can be expected to be playing survival poker and will therefore be vulnerable to a raise. However, sound judgment is required. Your raise might force a player who is in the blind to call because he feels he must defend his blind on the hand in question in order to have any further chance in the

tournament. Therefore, since you have nothing in the pot at the time, it will probably not be in your best interest to force one of the blinds to defend against you with a hand that is superior to the hand that you are holding "hot and cold." That is a hand that is better than yours given no betting after the early rounds.[3] This is especially true if you are on a short stack yourself. However, if the other players are not calling enough and your hand does have legitimate value, this is an excellent opportunity to take advantage of their tight play. (Probably the best time to try to steal the blinds is when you have a decent size stack of chips and the blinds stacks are small but not tiny.)

---

[3]A hand that is better "hot and cold," but not better if there are bets on each round would be a hand (assuming bets) that would tend to win a little for you when it finishes best, but would frequently loose a lot if your hand finishes second best.

Rebuys Revisited

In playing progressive stack rebuy tournaments, an intelligent rebuy strategy is critical to your long-term prospects for success. Here's a brief summary of recommended rebuy strategy for these tournaments.

1. **Limit tournaments.** Assuming the rebuy period lasts an hour, try to avoid making rebuys during the first forty minutes of play —especially the first twenty minutes of play — where you will be paying a premium for the chips. After the first forty minutes of play, make rebuys and add-on whenever you are eligible to do so since the chips will now be sold at a reduced price. This recommendation is based on the assumption that with maximum betting limits of only $30 and $60 prior to the end of the rebuy period, it is highly unlikely that you will have accumulated such a large stack that you should pass on the opportunity to purchase additional chips (at the reduced price).

2. **No-limit tournaments.** Same as the recommendation above except that you may wish to pass on the add-on option if you have accumulated a huge stack. For example, in a recent tournament, my stack at the intermission had grown from $200 in tournament chips to almost $6,000. What was the point of adding on an additional $400 in tournament chips? Clearly, this relatively small amount would have only a negligible impact on my chances of winning the tournament and would not be worth the cost of the rebuy. I refused the add-on option and ended the tournament with a negotiated three-way chop of the money remaining in the tournament pool.

So what constitutes a "huge" stack? That depends on many factors that are far too numerous and complex to adequately address here. In the very rare instances when you find yourself in this fortunate situation, check the size of other stacks in the tournament, especially at your table before making a decision. In general, I will consider refusing the add-on option only if I will still have a comfortable chip lead at my table even after all others have made the add-on. So, for the example above, this means an add-on is probably correct even if I have as much as $4,000 in tournament chips. From a purely financial perspective, this may not always be a profitable investment. However, if I do make the rebuy, and it is wrong, the most this error can cost me is the price of the rebuy which in our model tournament would be $10. When my rebuy decision is wrong, it isn't costing me that much.

The Ultimate Recommendation

If you are playing to win (and who isn't), never enter a progressive stack rebuy tournament unless you have both the resources and the intention to take advantage of all rebuy and add-on options. You will be at a significant disadvantage to those players who are prepared to make the proper rebuys if you choose not to. Although miracles do sometimes happen, you will not maximize your long term results if you are paying a higher price for your chips than your rivals. Furthermore, by not making the proper rebuys and add-on, you will quickly become a short stack which will put you into a survival mode early producing a strategic disadvantage against players with larger stacks.

The one exception is for freeroll tournaments that do not have an entry fee. However, for most freeroll tournaments, the rebuy stacks are far more progressive. For the last such tournament that I entered, the initial stack was $200 in tournament chips and the rebuy stacks increased to $500 and $1,000. For a tournament such as this, the first rebuy should be considered to be equivalent to the buy-in.

Common Mistakes

A number of mistakes are commonly made by players in progressive stack rebuy tournaments. Here they are, ranked in order of relative frequency.

1. Playing too loosely in the early stage of the tournament when the rebuy stack is still at the minimum level.

2. Not taking advantage of the tight play that always follows the end of the rebuy period.

3. Not properly adjusting starting hand requirements as the number of players at a table declines, and not taking into account the fact that some weak hands might be better than yours "hot and cold." (See the chapter entitled "Playing Short-Handed Poker" in Part Seven of this book.)

4. Not making a rebuy whenever eligible to do so after the rebuy stack has increased to the maximum level.

5. Entering a tournament with inadequate resources to take advantage of all rebuy and add-on options.

6. Purchasing additional chips at a premium price when not yet necessary to make a rebuy. For example, some players will make a rebuy just before the rebuy stack increases because they do not feel that they have adequate chips in their stack to play the next hand.

7. Going all-in when not necessary to do so, just before an increase in the rebuy stack.

8. Not taking full advantage of tight play by players who have short stacks (but not tiny stacks) near the end of the tournament.

9. Failing to avoid a confrontation with another player who has a large stack in the late stages of a tournament. This is, without a doubt, the most expensive single mistake that a player can make and it is sometimes made even by seasoned professionals. Usually this mistake is the result of a player thinking he has an overwhelming advantage that he loses sight of the fact that he is not playing at an open table, but in a tournament. If you have a large stack in the late stage of a tournament, never get into a raising war with another player with a large stack unless you are virtually certain you have the winning hand. The fact that you think you have the best hand going to the river is usually not adequate. You must have the "virtual nuts."

10. Not properly considering the small incremental cost of making a call in an unraised pot from the small blind. In most cases, the small blind is one-half the big blind. For example, if the big blind is $10, the small blind is $5. In some cases however, the small blind is two-thirds the big blind. For example, with a big blind of $15, the small blind is usually $10. Many small tournament players fail to recognize the significance of this difference.

    For example, in the standard structure where the small blind is one-half the big blind, you would frequently call an unraised pot from the small blind with a hand as weak as but nothing weaker. In the other structure, where the small blind is two-thirds the size of the big blind, an

could suffice in the same situation.

Against only the big blind, if you are in the small blind position, which requires you to double the amount of the small blind in order to call, you will be getting 3-to-1 odds on your call. If it is necessary to put in only an additional 50 percent of the small blind, you will be getting odds of 5-to-1 on your call. So call liberally here unless the player in the big blind is prone to raise.

In a multiway hand that has not been raised and with a player in the big blind who rarely raises, it is highly unlikely that you will have cards that would not justify a call if all you need to do is add 50 percent of your small blind. Yet, in this situation, I see many players fold their hands.

11. Failing to recognize the importance of position at the last table when many players are playing with short stacks.

12. Slowplaying friends at the table. (Not only is this bad strategy, it is also very poor poker etiquette.)

13. Failing to put an opponent all-in during the last stages of a tournament due to not being aware of that player's chip position.

14. Playing down a stack for too large an amount in order to qualify to make an additional rebuy.

15. Playing desperation poker with mediocre starting hands in an attempt to build a large stack prior to the end of the rebuy period.

Part Two

No Rebuy Tournaments

No Rebuy Tournaments

Introduction

Many players feel that the "cheap" progressive stack rebuy tournaments aren't so cheap. In fact, they claim they can be quite expensive. These players point out when you total up all the rebuys and add-ons these "small" events can be quite costly — and in some cases they are right.

They also argue, somewhat correctly, that the progressive stack rebuy tournaments favor the individual with "deep pockets." Having the ability to make many rebuys will allow someone to play more aggressively than the player who must conserve his chips from the beginning.

So this brings us to the "No Rebuy Tournaments," which are also very popular. Some of the concepts of the rebuy tournaments that we just discussed apply here, but take note: many other important strategic ideas are different.

Overview

No rebuy tournaments appear to be the second most popular type of small-stakes tournaments conducted in our casinos. For the most part, they seem to be popular in the smaller casinos and cardrooms. (At the other end of the scale, ironically, the major events like the World Series of Poker are also comprised mostly of no rebuy tournaments.)

From the management perspective, the primary advantage of these tournaments is that since the participants cannot rebuy, they become more readily available to play at an open table where collections can be made. The major disadvantage is that without rebuys it is more difficult to build tournament pools large enough to attract players. As a compromise, the buy-in for most no rebuy tournaments is generally higher than for rebuy tournaments.[4] In addition, in order to make the tournament more attractive, some casinos add a small amount of money to the tournament pool or guarantee a minimum for the tournament pool. (This guarantee is not as good as it sounds since some cardrooms have been known to quickly cancel their tournaments if poor attendance is forcing them to "ante up.")

An important characteristic of no rebuy tournaments distinguishing them from rebuy tournaments is that the initial stack is usually much larger in relation to the size of the opening bet. In a typical progressive stack rebuy tournament discussed in the previous chapter, the initial stack was only $200 in tournament chips and the limits increased to $30 and $60 after only forty minutes of play. Therefore, if rebuys were not permitted, the tournaments would be practically over after an hour of play. Clearly, this will not do. Casino managers, are aware that their

---

[4] Of course, if you consider the rebuys and add-ons, this may not be the case.

customers need to feel that they are getting value for their investment. Thus the tournament needs to last for more than an hour for most participants.

Following is an example of a small-stakes no rebuy tournament that I recently played. This is fairly typical of small-stakes tournaments of this type:

1. Buy-in: $20 (no service charge)

2. Buy-in stack: $1,000

3. Betting limits:

Betting Limits	
15 minutes	$15-$30
15 minutes	$30-$60
15 minutes	$50-$100
15 minutes	$100-$200
15 minutes	$200-$400
Intermission	
15 minutes	$300-$600
15 minutes	$500-$1,000
15 minutes	$1,000-$2,000
15 minutes	$2,000-$4,000
15 minutes	$3,000-$6,000

4. Tournament pool: $940

5. Tournament payout:

Tournament Payouts	
Place	Payout
1	40%
2	23%
3	12%
4	9%
5	6%
6	5%
7	3%
8	2%

The First Thirty Minutes

Because the betting limits seem very insignificant in relation to the initial stack, typically $1,000 in tournament chips, you can expect to see some extremely loose play in the opening stages. If you are looking for long-term success, do not join in this folly. Instead, get into the habit of playing solid, sensible poker and take advantage of the loose play of others, bearing in mind that at these levels of antes and blinds, you cannot hurt your stack by being patient. However, the "live" play that you will be against will sometimes provide you with an opportunity to build your stack and get a chip lead with little risk to your own initial stack. Notice that in this instance, we are taking advantage of opponents who play too many hands and go too far with their hands, rather than taking advantage of opponents who are playing too tight. In any poker environment, you should take note of how the other players at your table are playing and adjust accordingly.

By "solid, sensible poker," I do not mean to suggest that you should play very tight and only play premium hands. Far from it. In any poker environment, if you want to be a winner, you must tailor your play to meet that environment. In the early stages of a small-stakes tournament, the action is almost always very loose. In general, people who are playing this way are playing very poorly. In the long run, the way to beat people who are playing poorly is to play well. So relax your starting hand requirements as appropriate for a loose game.

In a game such as hold 'em, look for hands such as small pairs, medium suited connectors, and ace-little suited that you might readily discard at an open table, especially if you are in an early position. Even if there is a raise ahead of you, some of these hands, (particularly the small pairs) become playable if you can anticipate enough multiway action.

For example, if a tight player raises from an early position, a hand as weak as

may be playable if you can anticipate that several other players will automatically call. If you now hit your hand — that is, you flop a set — small pairs have the potential to provide a big payoff.

However, it would still be wrong to play a hand like

in this situation since your implied odds will probably not be high enough. With a hand like this, if you flop a draw you may be required to call bets and raises on both the flop and the turn in an attempt to hit your hand.

In the early stages of a stud tournament, small pairs, (particularly if they are buried), small three flushes, and three cards to a straight with a gap may be profitable, especially if you can get in for only the bring-in and your cards are live.

For example, if no one has yet raised and you hold a hand like

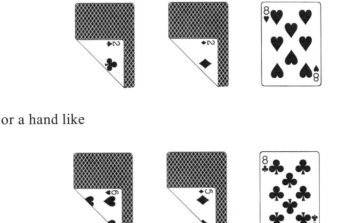

or a hand like

you can call providing that the cards you need, particularly the deuces in the first example and the sevens in the second example, are not out on board in other players' hands. You are looking to catch perfect. If you catch a "blank" and are facing a full bet on fourth street you should usually fold.

Another part of your strategy, especially if you are in an early position, is to use the check-raise more liberally. This is especially true in hold 'em. For example, if you are in an early position with a hand like

the flop comes

and you can anticipate a bet from an aggressive player in late position, you should go for the check-raise. This way you may be able to knock someone out who otherwise would call your bet and be getting proper odds to do so considering that you only have one pair.

If you are in a late position, be more inclined to slowplay a monster in the hope that you might be able to benefit from a loose bet after the betting limit doubles, providing the pot is not too big. If on the other hand the pot is large, go ahead and collect those early calls.

A word of caution however. Do not fall victim to a fairly common tendency to assume that an opponent does not have a very strong hand just because he has been betting and raising wildly. Players who play poorly in that manner often "seem" to be luckier than players who play tight. Such players are more proficient at getting themselves into a position to get lucky. The obvious reason is that by playing more hands, these loose players can be expected to draw out more often and more cards can make their hand.

Some players will argue that loose play in the early stages of a tournament is justified because it misleads other players who are in the tournament. Others argue that to play loosely early in a tournament is proper strategy because if you get lucky early on it can reduce the luck factor later because of your superior chip position. There is probably some justification for this but it is largely faulty reasoning. With the rapid changes in the betting limits and the composition of players at the table, there is precious little time in these small-stakes tournaments to fool anyone but yourself. In the long run, over a period of many tournaments, you can not afford to waste chips. However, playing a little looser trying to get lucky and therefore reduce the luck factor later on does make some sense, especially if the overall game is loose. This is why I recommend hands like small pairs in hold 'em and one-gap three-card straights in seven-card stud, especially if you can get in cheaply. However, this strategy can only be correct if your chip position is far away from being broke.

Many people who play in these small-stakes no rebuy tournaments on a regular basis lack a game plan for the early stages of the tournament. What should be your primary objective in the early minutes of play? Should it be to knock rivals out of the tournament whenever you have the opportunity to do so, or should priority be given to building your stack? Quite clearly, priority should be given to building your stack because at this stage of the tournament the value of all chips is still relatively constant.

Let's look at an example. Assume that the event is still in the second level of play and all entries are still in the tournament. The game is hold 'em and Player A is first to act. He bets $60 after the river card and has only $25 left in his stack. It is therefore virtually certain that he will call any raise.

Assume that you are the next to act and are holding a straight flush, the absolute nuts. However, there are still four other players who have yet to act. Would it be correct to raise in order to knock Player A out of the tournament? Probably not. At this stage it makes little difference whether all players are still alive (including Player A with only $25 in chips) or if there is one casualty. The reason is that at this moment the value of your stake is essentially a function of the size of your stack in relation to the total number of chips in the tournament, not the number of players remaining in the tournament.

Obviously, however, in the later stage of the tournament, knocking another player out can become the primary objective. For example, if there are only three players remaining, you can insure yourself of at least a second place finish by knocking a player out. The reason why this change in playing strategy occurs is that as the end of the tournament approaches, as mentioned previously, the value of a chip will vary, depending on the number of chips in a player's stack.

The larger the player's stack, the less each chip in that stack is actually worth and conversely, the smaller a player's stack the greater the value of each chip in that stack. Thus your strategy should include the proper plays to use this change to your advantage where it is appropriate to do so. (This, however, is not true in those rare tournaments that don't play down to the end or where everyone keeps what they have in front of them.)

The Second Thirty Minutes

During the second thirty-minute period (which is the third level of stakes — usually $50-$100), especially near the end of this time interval, the field will begin to thin very quickly due to attrition. Usually, however, if you have been playing as recommended here, there should be no immediate threat.

Be aware that due to the size of the limits in relation to the number of chips in the tournament, many players will be forced to defend blinds with hands that they might otherwise abandon. You should therefore be prepared to adjust your own starting hand requirements as might be appropriate. For example, in hold 'em, it might not be correct strategy to try a steal if you are the first in from a late position with a hand like

if you believe one of the blinds will automatically call. On the other hand, a holding like

may become a raising hand (as opposed to a fold) since with no betting, a king will sometimes win by itself without further improvement.

Also, be cognizant of the fact that many players enter these small-stakes no rebuy tournaments with the attitude that since it is cheap to enter the tournament, they will just "give it a shot." Therefore, once they get involved in a hand, they seem to have a tendency to hang in there to the bitter end. Obviously, it will be very difficult to run a bluff on such a player. When playing a tournament, look for players who have this mentality, especially among the unfamiliar faces.

The End Game

For most small-stakes no rebuy tournaments, the end game will begin almost immediately after the intermission because the size of the betting limits in relation to the total number of chips in the tournament will put many players in immediate danger of elimination. Your strategy, depending on your situation, should be as follows.

1. **You have one of the large stacks.** As in Part One, concentrate on eliminating players who have small stacks, especially if they are in the blinds and are clearly trying to survive so that they can reach the money. If another player with a large stack bets into you, do not get into a raising war with him until you are virtually certain that you have the winning hand. Keep in mind that with a large stack you should be able to finish in the money by just playing conservatively. But another player with a large stack might be able to eliminate you from the tournament with one big hand. A player with a short stack cannot.

   There is, of course, another reason why you as a player with a large stack should prefer to go up against a player with a small stack. As was mentioned earlier, his penalty for losing the pot will be more than yours. Also, my comments in Part One regarding how to play when you only have "way the best of it" and are against another player with a large stack apply here as well.

2. **You have a medium size stack.** You are probably not in immediate danger of elimination. Try to avoid confrontations with players who have larger stacks unless you feel that you have a clear advantage and concentrate on the smaller stacks. If you do decide to commit yourself to a promising hand, do

so decisively and aggressively with the attitude that you are going to position yourself to win the tournament. Good poker often dictates that you act decisively. By betting or raising you give your opponent a chance to fold. However, if the hand appears to go sour and you can save a few chips, you should always do so because as long as you still have a chip, you have a chance. (See the examples on pages 36 and 37..)

3. **You have one of the small stacks.** You will not have the luxury of waiting for a premium starting hand. In games that are played with blinds, the position of the dealer button is often far more important than the skill of the players. Pay close attention to its location and the stacks of players who will be required to post blinds before you. If they have small stacks, consider the possibility that you might be able to avoid posting blinds because of the movement of players and/or the consolidation of tables. If you do decide that you must commit yourself to a hand, do so aggressively. However, always bear in mind that if you can save even one chip, that might be enough to move you up the payout ladder.

Finally, to finish this section there are two ideas related to blind play that need to be mentioned. They are:

1. For games that are played with blinds, be aware that players with small stacks will often be forced to commit to less than ideal starting hands. So be prepared to stand your ground if you have a reasonable number of chips against players with small stacks who come on aggressively, especially if that player is in a position where he will soon be required to put up the big blind. (This concept is particularly true if you can easily put them all-in.)

By the same logic, if you see a player with a small stack bring it in for a raise and he has several hands to go before he is required to put up a blind, give him credit for a good hand.

In my experience, even in the smallest tournaments, few players play poorly enough to come out charging from a favorable position with a weak hand.

2. If you are in a late position, particularly if you are the dealer, the chip status of the two blinds becomes increasingly important. Almost all players with small stacks can be expected to be playing survival poker and will therefore be vulnerable to a raise. However, don't make this raise automatically. You might force a player who is in the blind to call because he feels that he must defend his blind in order to have any further chance in the tournament. This is particularly true if his stack is "tiny." Therefore, since you have nothing in the pot at the time, it will probably not be in your best interest to force one of the blinds to defend against you with a hand that is superior to the hand that you are holding "hot and cold." That is, a hand that is better than yours given no betting after the early rounds. This is especially true if you are on a short stack yourself. However, if the other players are not calling enough, and this will frequently be the case, and your hand does have legitimate value, keep in mind that this is an excellent opportunity to take advantage of their tight play. So again, the best time to steal the blinds is when you have a decent size stack and the blinds' stacks are small but not tiny.

Common Mistakes

A number of mistakes are commonly made by players in small-stakes no rebuy tournaments. They are listed as follows, approximately in order of relative frequency.

1. Playing too loosely in the early stage of the tournament because the limits seem insignificant in relation to the size of the initial stack.

2. Not properly adjusting starting hand requirements as the number of players at the table declines, and not taking into account the fact that some weak hands might be better than yours "hot and cold." For instance, king-nine offsuit is a favorite over eight-seven suited. (See the chapter entitled "Playing Short-Handed Poker" in Part Seven of this book.)

3. Not taking full advantage of the tight play of players who have short (but not tiny) stacks near the end of the tournament.

4. Failing to avoid a confrontation with another player who has a large stack in the late stages of the tournament. (See comments on page 44.)

5. Not properly considering the small incremental cost of making a call in an unraised pot from the small blind. (See comments and example on pages 44 and 45.)

6. Failing to recognize the importance of position at the last table when many players are playing with short stacks.

7. Slowplaying friends at the table. (Not only is this bad strategy, it is also very poor poker etiquette.)

8. Failing to put an opponent all-in in the late stages of a tournament due to not being aware of that player's chip position.

Part Three

Constant Stack Rebuy Tournaments

Constant Stack
Rebuy Tournaments

Introduction

Before Progressive Stack Rebuy Tournaments became popular, the most widely held type of tournament were the Constant Stack Rebuy Events. Today they have fallen somewhat out of favor at the smaller buy-ins because many players feel that it is a mistake for them to rebuy once the limits have been raised a couple of times. They believe that even with the rebuy they are just too much "out chipped."

This, however, is faulty reasoning. Even though your chances of winning the tournament have gone down, the rebuy is still usually profitable. (The reason for this is beyond the scope of this book. See *Gambling Theory and Other Topics* by Mason Malmuth.)

However, in the larger tournaments where rebuys are offered, they are almost always constant stack rebuy tournaments. Plus, not all small tournaments that offer rebuys are of the progressive nature. Thus, it is still very important to have a good understanding of appropriate strategy for these events.

Overview

Constant Stack Rebuy Tournaments differ from Progressive Stack Rebuy Tournaments (discussed in Part One of this book) in that the size as well as the cost of the rebuy stack remains unchanged throughout the rebuy period. The constant stack rebuy format is still popular for major tournaments, satellite tournaments, and special-event-type in-house tournaments with higher buy-ins. However, for small-stakes tournaments, they have been steadily overtaken by the progressive stack format.

The fact that rebuys are less attractive to many participants tends to limit the size of the tournament pools. To counter this, casinos introduced multiple simultaneous rebuys, but this led to the charge that it permits players with deep pockets to almost buy their way into the money. As a result, most Constant Stack Rebuy Tournaments now limit rebuys to one or two rebuys per player. In order to compensate for this limitation on rebuys and produce a large tournament prize pool, the buy-in and rebuy are usually higher than for Progressive Stack Rebuy Tournaments.

Following is an example of a typical Constant Stack Rebuy Tournament. Note that the initial stack is relatively large when compared to the Progressive Stack Rebuy Tournament ($500 in tournament chips versus $200 in tournament chips) but that the betting limits increase more rapidly. These are fairly common characteristics of small-stakes Constant Stack Rebuy Tournaments:

1.   Buy-in: $25 (including $5 service charge)

2.   Buy-in and rebuy stack: $500

3.   Number of players: 50-80

4.   Betting limits:

Betting Limits	
15 minutes	$10-$20
15 minutes	$15-$30
15 minutes	$30-$60
15 minutes	$50-$100
Intermission	
15 minutes	$100-$200
15 minutes	$200-$400
15 minutes	$350-$600
15 minutes	$500-$1,000
15 minutes	$1,000-$2,000
15 minutes	$2,000-$4,000

The First Thirty Minutes

Action in the early stages of a Progressive Stack Rebuy Tournament is usually very loose because it is cheap to make a rebuy. The same is true for No Rebuy Tournaments where the play is also usually very loose because the opening limits are small in relation to the size of the initial stacks.

The Constant Stack Rebuy Tournament is different in that the rebuy is generally more expensive than the Progressive Stack Rebuy Tournament and the initial stack is smaller than the No Rebuy Tournament. The result is that play in the early stages is usually somewhat more conservative than either of its counterparts.

Every major tournament I have ever seen that allows rebuys uses the constant stack format. It is common knowledge that the early action in a major tournament allowing rebuys is more aggressive than a no rebuy tournament. So why would the action be different for small-stakes tournaments? The answer undoubtedly lies in the structure of the tournaments. For small-stakes No Rebuy Tournaments, the opening limits are very small in relation to the size of the initial stack, but increase rapidly, usually every fifteen or twenty minutes.

For major No Rebuy Tournaments, the limits increase much more slowly, but the opening limits are usually of sufficient size to discourage excessive loose play. Obviously, the caliber and mentality of the players also have a bearing. In my experience, players in major tournaments are far less likely to play marginal hands just because the betting limits are relatively low. In other words, when compared to the average small-stakes tournament player, most major tournament players are much more conservative just as middle- and high-limit players tend to be more solid than those who play in the low-limit games.

While it is undoubtedly true that early play in a small-stakes Constant Stack Rebuy Tournament is usually more conservative than a Progressive Stack Rebuy Tournament or a No Rebuy Tournament, you should not get the impression that you can expect to find conservative play in the early stages of any small stakes tournament. It's all relative. In fact, even in the small-stakes Constant Stack Rebuy Tournaments, the early action is generally considerably more aggressive than at the average small-stakes table on the casino floor.

The recommended playing strategy for the first thirty minutes of play is therefore that you play solid, relatively conservative poker in order to take advantage of the loose play of others. This recommendation is also based on the fact that in the first thirty minutes of play, the tournament cannot be won, and it is very difficult to win a pot with less than the best hand

I do not mean to discourage creative play. However, make sure that you make the proper adjustments that were discussed previously for playing in loose games. This includes playing small pairs in hold 'em and one-gap three-card straights in unraised stud pots.

For Progressive Stack Rebuy Tournaments, it was recommended that you avoid making early rebuys because of the small size of early rebuy stacks. For Constant Stack Rebuy Tournaments, it is recommended that you make a rebuy whenever you are low on chips. In tournaments that pay a predetermined percentage to finalists, these rebuys will always have a positive expectation assuming of course that you are a competent player. Also, you want to insure that you always have sufficient chips in your stack so that you will be able to get maximum value on your winning hands.

Most writers on poker tournament strategy recommend that you play fast in the early stages of a Constant Stack Rebuy Tournament if you intend to rebuy. That will give you an excellent opportunity to build your stack. While I have no disagreement with those who advocate such a strategy, I do have reservations regarding the wisdom of such a strategy for some of the small-stakes tournaments that I have seen. In my personal experience, during the early stages of most small-stakes tournaments, there is so much loose play that it best suits my personal style of play to wait for a premium hand or a hand that has clear value for the particular situation. Needless to say, when good cards arrive, I hope to be there with plenty of chips to take maximum advantage of it. That is why you should make the appropriate adjustments for loose play and play those hands that have the potential to win a big pot. Now when you flop a set or make that unexpected straight or flush, you can collect a lot of chips.

The Second Thirty Minutes

During the second half of the rebuy period, many of the players who do not plan to rebuy will be forced to commit to a less than ideal hand because of the increase in the size of antes, blinds, and forced entry bets. If you have won your share of pots or made early rebuys as was suggested above, you should be able to take advantage of such players. Consider a raise in order to isolate a player who comes in with a short stack. For example, in hold 'em, you might consider a raise with

That is an ace with a marginal kicker. Notice that this is a hand that you might otherwise have considered folding. (Remember to consider the players behind you and the blinds.) Otherwise, continue to play poker well as if you were in a standard ring game.

As indicated earlier, in tournaments that pay a percentage, you should always make a rebuy when you are low on chips. Many otherwise good tournament players violate this principle, which we will now address.

If you already have a large stack, your expectation for an add-on may be negative. Even though the add-on may improve your chances of advancing to the payoff point, it may not be worth the price. The reason is that your last rebuy will go into the tournament pool, but you can only receive a percentage of the pool. For example, suppose that you have a huge stack but decide to make a $20 add-on. If it turns out that you would have won the tournament with a very high probability, even if you had not made the add-on, since you normally receive 40 percent of the tournament pool, the add-on will have cost you close to $12.

$$\$12 = (1 - 0.40)(\$20)$$

In practice however, it is probably unlikely that will find yourself in such a fortunate situation except in a no-limit tournament. Therefore, my recommendation is if you find yourself with a huge stack at the end of the rebuy period and still have a rebuy or add-on option, check the stacks of the other players before making your decision. Bear in mind that an additional add-on of typically $500 in tournament chips may help you survive to the payoff point, but it probably will not be a significant factor in negotiating a settlement at the last table.

Another factor that needs to be considered in any rebuy decision is the amount (if any) of funds that have been added to the tournament pool by the sponsoring casino, either by a direct subsidy or a guarantee. If the amount that has been added is significant, I would recommend that you exercise all rebuy/add-on options regardless of the size of your stack. (However, in my experience, the amount that has been added is usually relatively insignificant and the long-term impact of such subsidies is minimal because such subsidies rarely continue over an extended period of time.)[5]

---

[5] At the time of this writing, an exception is occurring on some Internet sites which are trying to attract business.

The Intermediate Stage

In Part One, the intermediate stage of a rebuy tournament was defined as that time interval from the end of the rebuy period to the point at which players begin to be concerned about the number of players remaining in the tournament. For a Progressive Stack Rebuy Tournament, the intermediate stage usually ends more than an hour after the end of the rebuy period. For Constant Stack Rebuy Tournaments, the intermediate stage will end much sooner, usually only fifteen to thirty minutes after the end of the rebuy period. The reason is that there are usually considerably fewer rebuys and the rebuy stacks are smaller.

As in any rebuy tournament, there is a natural tendency for the action to slow down immediately following the end of the rebuy period. However, in most small-stakes Constant Stack Rebuy Tournaments, this lull is usually very short lived because the blinds and betting limits rise rapidly and quickly put all but a few players in imminent danger of elimination. As in any situation where there are a lot of players who will be playing survival poker, try to take advantage of tight play by being more aggressive yourself, especially when you are in a late position and/or are against players with short (but not tiny) stacks. However, as before, keep in mind that if a short stack raises from a position where they still have several hands to play before the blinds, you are more likely to be looking at a quality hand.

The End Game

End game strategy for Constant Stack Rebuy Tournaments is essentially the same as Progressive Stack Rebuy Tournaments or No Rebuy Tournaments. So if you are already familiar with what has already been written, you may want to skip this chapter. If you choose to go ahead and read this, depending on your situation, your strategy should be as follows.

1.   **You have one of the large stacks.** As before, concentrate on eliminating players who have small stacks especially if they are in the blinds and are clearly trying to survive so that they can reach the money. If another player with a large stack bets into you, do not get into a raising war with him until you are virtually certain that you have the winning hand. Keep in mind that with a large stack, you should be able to at least finish in the money by just playing conservatively. But another player with a large stack might be able to eliminate you from the tournament with one big hand. A player with a short stack cannot.

   There is, of course, another reason why you as a player with a large stack should prefer to go up against a player with a small stack. As was mentioned earlier, his penalty for losing the pot will be more than yours. Also, my comments in Part One regarding how to play when you only have "way the best of it" and are against another player with a large stack apply here as well.

2.   **You have a medium size stack.** You are probably not in immediate danger of elimination. Try to avoid confrontations with players who have larger stacks unless you feel that you have a clear advantage and concentrate on the smaller stacks. If you do decide to commit yourself to a promising hand, do

so decisively and aggressively with the attitude that you are going to position yourself to win the tournament with this hand. Good poker often dictates that you act decisively. By betting or raising you give your opponent a chance to fold. However, if the hand appears to go sour and you can save a few chips, you should always do so because as long as you still have a chip, you still have a chance. (See the examples on pages 36 and 37.)

3. **You have one of the small stacks.** You will not have the luxury of waiting for a premium starting hand. In games that are played with blinds, the position of the dealer button is often far more important than the skill of the players. Pay close attention to its location and the stacks of players who will be required to post blinds before you. If they have small stacks, consider the possibility that you might be able to avoid posting blinds because of the movement of players and/or the consolidation of tables. If you do decide that you must commit yourself to a hand, do so aggressively. However, always bear in mind that if you can save even one chip, that might be enough to move you up the payout ladder.

Finally, to finish this section there are two ideas related to blind play that needs to be mentioned. They are:

1. For games that are played with blinds, be aware that players with small stacks will often be forced to commit to less than ideal starting hands. So be prepared to stand your ground if you have a reasonable number of chips against players with small stacks who come on aggressively, especially if that player is in a position where he will soon be required to put up the big blind. (This concept is particularly true if you can easily put them all-in.)

By the same logic, if you see a player with a small stack bring it in for a raise and he has several hands to go before he is required to put up a blind, give him credit for a good hand. In my experience, even in the smallest tournaments, few players play poorly enough to come out charging from a favorable position with a weak hand.

2. If you are in a late position, particularly if you are the dealer, the chip status of the two blinds becomes increasingly important. Almost all players with small stacks can be expected to be playing survival poker and will therefore be vulnerable to a raise. However, don't make this raise automatically. You might force a player who is in the blind to call because he feels that he must defend his blind in order to have any further chance in the tournament. This is especially true if his stack is "tiny." Therefore, since you have nothing in the pot at the time, it will probably not be in your best interest to force one of the blinds to defend against you with a hand that is superior to the hand that you are holding "hot and cold." That is, a hand that is better than yours given no betting after the early rounds. This is especially true if you are on a short stack yourself. However, if the other players are not calling enough and this will frequently be the case, and your hand does have legitimate value, keep in mind that this is an excellent opportunity to take advantage of their tight play. So again, the best time to steal the blinds is when you have a decent size stack and the blinds stacks are small but not tiny.

Common Mistakes

A number of common mistakes are often made by players in small-stakes Constant Stack Rebuy Tournaments. They are listed as follows, approximately in the order of relative frequency.

1. Playing too loosely in the early stages of the tournament.

2. Not taking advantage of tight play that always follows the end of the rebuy period.

3. Not properly adjusting starting hand requirements as the number of players at the table declines and not taking into account the fact that some weak hands might be better than yours "hot and cold." (See the chapter entitled "Playing Short-Handed Poker" in Part Seven of this book.)

4. Failing to make a rebuy when low on chips. This is important because in tournaments that pay a predetermined percentage to finalists, these rebuys will always have positive expectation providing you are a competent player.

5. Entering a tournament with inadequate resources to properly take advantage of all rebuy and add-on options.

6. Not taking full advantage of tight play by players who have short stacks near the end of the tournament.

7. Failing to avoid a confrontation with another player who has a large stack in the late stages of the tournament. (See comments on page 44.)

8. Not properly considering the small incremental cost of making a call in an unraised pot from the small blind. (See comments and example on page ???.)

9. Failing to recognize the importance of position at the last table when many players are playing with short stacks.

10. Slowplaying friends at the table. (Not only is this bad strategy, it is also very poor poker etiquette.)

11. Failing to put an opponent all-in near the end of the tournament due to not being aware of that player's chip position.

Part Four

Sudden Sayonara Tournaments

Sudden Sayonara Tournaments

Introduction

A big complaint of many tournament players and tournament directors regards the length of tournaments: Some just last too long. This is particularly true if some of the players who make the final table are very conservative.

One solution is to end the tournament before all the players have been eliminated. Now both the tournament director and the last remaining players can get a good night's sleep.

Overview

A Sudden Sayonara Tournament is an event that ends abruptly when the number of players remaining declines to a predetermined number. Usually, that number is three or four — and only those players who survived to the end of the tournament share in the tournament pool. Although the sudden sayonara format is now relatively rare, these tournaments do seem to crop up from time to time, especially in the smaller cardrooms and casinos where the number of tournament players is small.

At the end of the tournament, chips are counted, and one of the following methods is used to determine amounts that will be paid to the finalists:

1. **Predetermined percentage method.** The amounts to be paid to the final players are determined in advance as a percentage of the total amount of money in the tournament pool. For example, if four players are to share in the money, usually 50 percent will be paid for first place, 25 percent for second place, 15 percent for third place, and 10 percent for fourth place. (However, I have also seen tournaments that paid 40, 30, 20, and 10 percent respectively. This latter distribution would appear to be much more equitable.)

2. **Chip count ratio method.** Amounts to be paid to the final players are based on the percentage of the total chips that each player has after the last hand of the tournament has been played. In other words, if Player A has 95 percent of the tournament chips, he will receive 95 percent of the money in the tournament pool.

Strategy

Advanced knowledge of which method of payment will be used can be a critical factor in determining correct strategy for the last few hands of the tournament. For example, assume that there are five players remaining in a tournament that will end when there are only four players remaining. In other words, when one more player is eliminated, the tournament will be over. Further assume that the last five players have the following quantities of chips:

Player A	$40,000
Player B	$39,000
Player C	$39,100
Player D	$38,000
Player E	$1,000

If the chip count ratio method is used and either Player A, B, C, or D eliminate Player E in heads-up play on the next hand, it is fairly obvious that the last four players will share in the tournament pool on a fairly equal basis.

However, if the predetermined percentage method is used, the potential payout picture changes completely because if Player C is the player that eliminates Player E, he will win the tournament and probably receive 50 percent of the tournament pool in spite of the fact that he will end the tournament with only $100 more in tournament chips than Player A and $200 more than Player B. On the other hand, if Player D is the player that eliminates Player E, it will actually amount to a "bad beat" for Player D because he would receive only 10 percent of the tournament pool in spite of the fact that he will end the tournament with 24.7 percent of the chips. In such a situation, it would clearly be in Player D's best interest to allow Player E to survive the hand, especially if the game being played uses blinds because Player D would have much to gain (an additional 40 percent of the tournament pool) and little to lose.

For example, with the distribution of chips indicated above, assume that Player E is in the big blind position for $1,000 in tournament chips and Player D is in the small blind for $500. If Players A, B, and C have all folded, Player D should fold even if he has

However, if there has been at least one call, Player D should raise because he would now be in a position to win the tournament by winning this hand.

Thus, this is an example of a situation in which it would be proper strategy to fold an extremely strong starting hand that would have been a heavy favorite to win the pot. Situations also occur when it might be correct to call with an extremely weak starting hand that would appear to be a prohibitively large underdog. For example, assume that instead of the chip counts shown above, the last five players had the following quantities of tournament chips:

Player A	$40,000
Player B	$5,000
Player C	$38,000
Player D	$500
Player E	$1,000

Further assume that:

1. Player A, who is known as a rock, has raised to $2,000
2. Player B has folded
3. Player C's pocket cards are

4. Player D is the small blind and is all-in for $500
5. Player E is the big blind and is all-in for $1,000

and that Player C realizes that his 7♥2♣ is the worst possible starting hand to be playing in a four-way pot that has been raised by a tight player who must have a good hand.

What would be the proper course of action for Player C? He should call the raise because it is almost certain that this will be the last hand of the tournament, and Player C is virtually assured of at least a second place finish. However, if by some miracle he should win this pot, he would win the tournament.

In the two examples discussed above, the chip distribution of the last five players was exaggerated in order to simplify explanations. In practice such extreme distributions are relatively rare. However, in the last stages of a Sudden Sayonara Tournament, similar although less extreme situations frequently do occur. Therefore, at the end of these tournaments, it is extremely important to understand the payout distribution and keep informed about the chip position of the other players. The rewards for having this knowledge and knowing how to use it can be quite substantial.

On the other hand, when you keep what you have in front of you the proper strategy is exactly the same as a ring game except that you would adjust to other players playing differently than normal because they don't realize this.

Part Five

Shootout Tournaments

Shootout Tournaments

Introduction

Shootout tournaments are events where the tables are not consolidated, but where each table is played down to one person who then advances to the final table.

A typical advertisement for a shootout tournament may say something like "You only have to beat sixteen players to win." This would refer to your opponents at the first table and your opponents at the second table assuming a nine-handed game. In reality, it is as difficult to win a shootout tournament as it would be any other. On the other hand, they are a "change of pace" and can be fun to play, especially if you enjoy short-handed poker.

Overview

Shootout tournaments are No Rebuy Tournaments in which play at each table continues until one player has won all the chips. This winner then advances to the next round of play. Although these shootout tournaments were fairly popular in casinos a few years ago, they are relatively rare today. That's because the format has never been well liked by players or management.

From a management perspective, shootout tournaments are not looked upon with favor because they tend to tie down too many tables and dealers for an extended period of time. Another drawback is that shootout tournaments are difficult to administer because, in order to be fair to all players, the same number of players would be required at all tables. This always presents a problem because tournament players are notorious stragglers, and management never knows how many late arrivals they are going to have. Obviously, this problem could be alleviated if the tournaments were started on time.

A possible solution would be to discontinue signing additional players whenever management feels that they can no longer complete an additional table. However, refusing to accept late arrivals is an act that evidently runs contrary to the nice guy image that tournament directors like to cultivate.

Shootout tournaments were never popular with players because some tables will invariably complete play much faster than others. The result is a long wait for some first-table winners. Another drawback in the eyes of many players is that more often than not, winners at the first tables will agree to a chop. It is relatively easy to reach agreement prior to the start of the second session because each surviving player will begin the second session with a stack of equal size. However, if the tournament pool is going to be chopped anyway, why make players wait around until the final first-table winner is determined?

The First Table

Strategy for playing the first table of a shootout tournament is the essence of simplicity. There is no need to consider such factors as rebuy or survival strategy. All you need to do is concentrate on eliminating all other players at your table since the first table is essentially winner-take-all.

Although there is no need to push the panic button in the opening minutes of play, be cognizant of the fact that betting limits will be increasing very rapidly. If you decide to play a hand, do so aggressively. Be inclined to bet your hand for value and otherwise press any advantage that you think you have.

As we mentioned in the introduction, this book was written with the assumption that the reader is a competent poker player. Therefore, the real key to success at the first table is the ability to make proper adjustments as the number of players at your table declines. Any competent hold 'em player is aware that at a full table, an

is a very weak hand if you are the first player to act before the flop. At what point (number of players) is the A♣9♠ strong enough to warrant a raise? In lowball poker, a one-card draw to a nine such as is also a very weak hand at a full table if you are the first player in. At what point is this a strong starting hand? For a discussion of strategy for playing short-handed poker, see the chapter entitled "Playing Short Handed Poker" in Part Seven of this book.

In the experience of the author, because of the small amount of money involved, there is little incentive to cut a deal at the first table. Therefore, since being the first player to be eliminated at your table is really no different than being the last player to be eliminated, be aggressive with the hands that you choose to play. Due to the fact that there is going to be only one winner at your table, which means that the chips do not change value, survival is not a consideration. Be inclined to press any small advantage you might have just as you would in a regular ring game in order to get the maximum return on every potential winning hand. However, this should not be construed as a suggestion that you should charge blindly ahead once you get involved in a hand. As in any poker environment, there is always room for sound judgment and a knowledge of your opponent. In other words, as in any other poker situation, you must play your hands well.

The Second Session

The second session of a small-stakes Shootout Tournament (if played) will almost always begin with a short table because the number of entrants to these tournaments is rarely adequate to provide for eight or nine full tables. Therefore, since skill at playing short-handed is the key element, your attention is again directed to the "Playing Short-Handed Poker" chapter in Part Seven of this book.

The second session of a Shootout Tournament is unique in that this is the only situation in tournament play where players will begin play in a late stage of a tournament all having stacks of equal size. Therefore, at least for the opening minutes of play, the recommendations previously stated in this text on how to play with various stack sizes are not relevant. There are, however, some clues about what you can expect from the other players as play begins (in the second session).

As a rule, the players (usually there will not be more than one or two) who will not agree to a chop will probably not be playing conservative, survival poker. This is not to suggest that the player(s) in question will come out charging like "maniacs." However, it is my experience that most players who will not agree to a chop when all players have stacks of equal size tend to be aggressive players. The exception might be the "rock" who thinks that he is a superior player and can outplay the others at the table. In my experience, however, the truly superior poker player who would be willing to spend the four or five hours needed to play out one of these small-stakes shootout tournaments is extremely rare.

In general, players who were in favor of a chop can be expected to be a fairly conservative bunch who will open play cautiously and try to move up the ladder. The rare exception is the player who might have gone on tilt because his offer to chop was rejected.

There is one last observation about these small-stakes shootout tournaments. There seems to be a tendency among players who favor making a deal to try to "get" the renegade so that they can then proceed with the chop. This may or may not work to the detriment of the renegade. If the renegade is aware of this, he might be able to use this knowledge to his advantage. And if this does happen, whether you are the renegade or not, you should be able to use this to your own advantage.

Part Six

Last Table Negotiations

Last Table Negotiations

Introduction

One very important aspect of tournament play doesn't even involve playing. It is what is known as last table negotiations. Even though most tournaments appear to have a winner, the fact of the matter is that much of the prize money has been predecided before the last hand has been dealt. That is, the last remaining players make a deal.

This type of deal making, like most types of deal making, is both an art and a science. Many players don't understand the true value of their situations, while others are more interested in a trophy than the money. You, as the skillful tournament player and deal maker, can use these opportunities to take advantage of your opponents, just like you do in all other aspects of poker.

Overview

Because of the size of the blinds and betting limits in relation to the number of chips in the tournament, action among the last few players in a small-stakes tournament usually degenerates into little more than a crap shoot, with most of the players only one or two hands away from elimination. In other words, luck not skill frequently determines the outcome. Because of the large differences in the amount of money that will be paid to the finalists, there is a great deal of incentive for the last few players remaining in the tournament to negotiate a mutually agreeable division of the money remaining in the tournament pool.

To determine how the last few players in a tournament might equitably "chop" the money, complex studies have been made based on mathematical probabilities. For any readers who might be interested in further details, I again refer you to *Gambling Theory and Other Topics* by Mason Malmuth or *Tournament Poker for Advanced Players* by David Sklansky. However, for our purposes, a few simple facts should suffice to equip the average small-stakes tournament player with the knowledge needed to negotiate equitable (if not more than equitable) settlements at the last table.

The Amount at Stake

Always bear in mind that the amount at stake (that is, the amount being negotiated) is not the total amount of money remaining in the tournament pool but some fraction of that amount. For example, if there are three players remaining in the tournament and these players will receive $600, $400 and $250, the amount that is being negotiated is not $1,250 but only $500. This is because each of the last three players has already won the $250 that will be paid for third place. It never fails to amaze me that some small tournament regulars still seem to have only a vague understanding of this simple concept.

Assume that with the payout shown above, Players A, B, and C have the following quantities of chips:

Player A	$100,000
Player B	$30,000
Player C	$900

The fact that Player C's meager stack of $900 is worth at least $250 and Player A can win only a maximum of $600 demonstrates an important concept of percentage payback tournaments, namely that the value of a chip in a large stack is lower than the value of a chip in a small stack. The moral? When negotiating a chop, don't sell yourself short just because you happen to have one of the small stacks, especially if you happen to have a favorable position relative to the blinds.

Another very important fact needs to be considered if you are one of the players with a small stack. Players with a big chip lead in the final stages of a tournament invariably seem to fall into one of two categories. There is the optimist who will figure that all he has to do is ram home his chip advantage and pick up all the marbles, and there is the pessimist who will feel that it would be a real shame if he fails to win the tournament after having such a huge lead. Oftentimes, the negotiating stance of the chip leader will be readily discernible from his response to the first offer to negotiate. Pay close attention because the pessimist is usually much more likely to agree to an offer that concedes him first place in the tournament for a favorable concession to players who have smaller stacks. Also, in my experience, women generally seem to be more inclined to agree to a chop than men. However, if a woman does not initially agree to a chop, you can usually assume that she will be more likely to stand her ground than a man, especially if the other finalists are all men, which is frequently the case. Presumably, this is because many women seem to be distrustful of a bunch of men who are trying to talk her into something.

When a settlement is made among the last few players, the usual method is to apportion the "amount at stake" according to the size of each player's stack. For example, assume that Players A, B, and C agree to a chop in a tournament that provides for payment of $1,000 for first place, $500 for second place, and $300 for third place, and that players A and B each have 30 percent of the chips and Player C has 40 percent. Since the "amount at stake" is $900 ($1,800 minus three times $300), players A and B would receive $570 each.

$$\$570 = \$300 + (0.30)(\$900)$$

Player C would receive $660.

$$\$660 = \$300 + (0.40)(\$900)$$

This formula works well if the stacks of the last few players are reasonably equal in size. However, if they are not, a problem arises. For example, if Player A has only 5 percent of the chips, the formula would call for him to receive only $345. Since he has already assured himself of at least $300, he could hardly be expected to give up the opportunity to win the $1,000. For only $45 more than the $300 that he has already won, especially if he is in a good position relative to the blinds, he still has a shot at first place. In instances such as this, it is the usual practice for players with a large stack to pay players with small stacks a premium. This is reasonable and fair because as we've previously noted, the value of a chip in a small stack is higher than the value of a chip in a large stack.

Another factor that should be noted is that if one of the players has a very large stack, rigid application of this formula would result in the payment of more than the actual amount of first place money to that person. For instance, if one of the players had 90 percent of the chips, rigid application of the formula would call for payment of $1,110

$$\$1,110 = \$300 + (0.90)(\$900)$$

in spite of the fact that, in the example, first place only pays $1,000.

The Position
of the Dealer Button

For games such as Omaha, hold 'em, and lowball, the position of the dealer button can be a critical factor, especially for players who advance to the last table with a short stack. This is especially true for lowball because lowball has only two rounds of betting, and the blinds usually constitute a much higher percentage of each pot than the other mentioned games.

If you advance to the final table with a small stack but get favorable position (such as the dealer position) do not sell yourself short. Due to the size of the blinds in relation to the total number of chips on the table, luck plays a huge role. In a game that is played with two blinds, from the dealer position you can usually count on seeing six or seven hands (assuming a full table) before being forced to commit any of your chips. This is a huge advantage over a player with a similar sized stack who will start play from the big blind position because one good hand could put you in a position to challenge the chip leaders. There is also the possibility that other players will be eliminated from the tournament before you will be required to post a blind.

The IRS

According to an IRS ruling, casinos are required to issue an IRS form W2-G to any payee who receives $600 or more at the end of a tournament. Most players would therefore prefer to receive $599 rather than $600. This creates opportunities for the knowledgeable. For instance, assume that players A, B, and C are the last three players remaining in a tournament that pays the top three finishers $900, $450, and $225. Further assume that players A and B have huge stacks of approximately equal size and that Player C, who has the big blind on the next hand, does not even have enough chips left to fully satisfy the big blind requirement.

If players A and B chop first and second place money, they will each receive $675 and the IRS form. Would they accept an offer to take $599 each and leave $377 for third place? In my experience, there are many players who will consider taking the $599 and leaving $377 for third place. As a result, Player C could leave the table with $377 rather than an almost certain $225. Situations such as this occur quite frequently in small-stakes tournaments. Be aware of them and be prepared to negotiate to your advantage. Also, for those of you new to poker tournaments, casino personnel will usually respect the wishes of the players as long as the arrangement is agreed to by all remaining players before the next hand is dealt.

The Skill of the Negotiators

In any negotiations, the knowledge and skill of the negotiators is crucial. As we indicated earlier, you will find that many of the finalists are not even certain of the actual amount of money that is at stake. Also, many finalists seem to have only a vague concept of how to equate the size of a stack to the value of that stack, and have a tendency to overvalue a large stack in relation to a small stack.

Here is another example. Suppose that Player A and Player B are the last two players in a tournament that will pay $1,000 for first place and $500 for second place. Further assume that Player A has 80 percent of the chips or a 4-to-1 advantage over Player B. In spite of his seemingly huge chip advantage, Player A's actual advantage in terms of value is only 50 percent. ($900 for Player A compared to $600 for Player B.) In order to compute the value of Player A's stack, simply add $400 (80 percent of the difference between first place money and second place money) to the $500 that Player A has already won.

Player A: $900 = $500 + (0.80)($500)

Player B: $600 = $500 + (0.20)($500)

In general, because unanimous agreement is necessary, it is difficult to reach agreement on a chop until the number of players remaining in the tournament declines to three or four. The exception is when the chip distribution is fairly even. Take note of which players seem to be eager to chop and which players are not. Again, as was stated earlier, players who are eager to chop will tend to play conservatively in order to survive. Players who do not want to chop will tend to be more aggressive. Look for any players who appear to have gone on tilt because their offer to chop has been rebuffed. Such a player may come out swinging — especially against those who have rebuffed him — even though the general tendency for players who want to chop is to be conservative.

Over the last few years, I have participated in many last table negotiations and can report to you with certainty that I have never witnessed an occasion in which a chop was agreed upon by players who were shouting at each other. Try to be diplomatic in these negotiations. You will be far more likely to succeed if you have a cordial relationship with the other players.

To some players, winning one of these tournaments is important as an ego booster. Be prepared to diplomatically concede such a player first place if they have the largest stack. However, be cognizant of the fact that such a player will often settle for little or no more money over a player with a smaller stack, especially if there is a photographer standing by to record the big event.

One last word of advice. When participating in one of these negotiations, never give the impression that you are eager to chop, especially if you really are. Obviously, if you have a small stack and an unfavorable position relative to the blinds, you will have little leverage with which to negotiate. If you have a decent stack, and/or a favorable position relative to the blinds, the other finalists will be much more inclined to give consideration to your views if they believe that you are amenable to an equitable chop but are also perfectly willing to continue play. (This may be a good time to promote the inaccurate formula accepted by many tournament players that we discussed earlier.) In other words, when negotiating, try to exhibit confidence, reasonableness, and especially restraint.

Part Seven

Other Topics

Other Topics

Introduction

Though we've covered the different strategies necessary to do well in the various kinds of tournaments we're still not quite there yet. There are a few more topics that need to be discussed to assure your long-term success: "Tournament Tie Breakers," "Playing Short-Handed Poker," and "The Collusion Stage."

Many of the better tournament players will tell you that one of the things that truly separates them from the "also rans" is the ability to play short-handed. Ring game players can always avoid short-handed play. All they have to do is quit the game.

Tournament players do not have this luxury. If you have chips you must play no matter how many empty seats there may be at your table. In addition, if you win the tournament you must triumph at the final table, which will become short-handed. Therefore, pay special attention to the chapter in this section on short-handed play. Many of you may want to read (and study) it several times.

Chip Exchanges

A chip exchange is the process of exchanging small denomination chips for larger denomination chips when the smaller denomination chips are being withdrawn from a tournament. Since chips are normally exchanged at least twice during the course of a tournament, knowledge of how you might benefit from these exchanges could give you an advantage over some of the other participants.

When a chip exchange is made, one of the following methods will be used:

1. **Par value plus any fraction exchange.** Chips being exchanged are exchanged at par value. In addition, a larger denomination chip is given for any fractions. In other words, if $5 chips are being withdrawn from the tournament and are being exchanged for $20 chips, players with five, six, seven, and eight $5 chips will receive two $20 chips. Notice that if the blinds are $10 and $20 and you are in the $10 blind position with seven or eight $5 chips, it will not cost you anything to make a call, provided that there has been no raise and the chip exchange will take place before you are again required to post a blind.

   This is a factor that many small tournament players fail to recognize. Don't be one of them. Although this may not seem very important, in the long run the player who knows how to tip the scales, however slightly, in his favor is going to have the advantage.

2. **Par value plus 50 percent exchange.** Chips that are being withdrawn are exchanged at par value. In addition, a larger denomination chip is given for fractions of one-half or more. Fractions of less than one-half are forfeited. In other words,

players with six, seven, eight, and nine $5 chips will receive two $20 chips. Therefore, for the same reason as Number 1 above, players who have eight or nine $5 chips and are in the small blind position may be able to get a free call.

3. **Race off.** Chips that are being withdrawn are exchanged at par value. All players at the table who have an odd number of chips remaining after the exchange draw cards for the remaining chips with one card being received for each odd chip. The player who draws the highest card by suit wins all of the odd chips at the table.

Note that at the time of the chip exchange, if a player has only the smallest denomination chips and the number of such chips in his possession is not adequate to receive at least one of the larger chips, there is a possibility that the player in question might be eliminated from the tournament without even being able to play a hand. Because of complaints from such players who had been eliminated from a tournament in this manner in the past, some tournament managers allow players who are in this situation one of the following options:

A. Participate in the race off in the normal manner or;

B. Exchange their smaller denomination chip (or chips) for one of the larger denomination chips.

When offered this second option, some players choose to participate in the race off because they believe that they will have no real chance in the tournament with only one chip. That is a mistake. As the late Jack Straus demonstrated years ago at the World Series of Poker, if you still have a "chip and a chair," you always have a chance to win it all. Never give up. Never!

If you have been given Option A or B, always take the chip because by doing so you will always be adding to the value of your stack. For example, if you have three $100 chips when the

$100 chips are being exchanged for $500 chips, you will be increasing your stack by $200. Surviving in a tournament in this manner can be especially important at the last table if you have a favorable position relative to the blinds because players who have small stacks will be required to post blinds before you will be required to commit your last chip.

Tournament Tie Breakers

When two or more players are eliminated from the tournament during the play of a hand, one of the following methods will usually be used in determining final tournament placing:

1. **Most chips method.** The player who had the most chips at the start of the last hand is considered to have been eliminated last and will receive the higher placing.

2. **Sharecropper method.** All players who were eliminated during the hand are considered to have tied.

Although the vast majority of tournament managers use the most chips method, you should always verify this fact beforehand because otherwise, the consequences of what may have seemed to have been a very routine play can turn out to be a disaster. As an example of such a situation, assume that it is the final stages of a seven-card stud tournament. You are one of four surviving players. However, only the last three players will share in the prize money which will be $600 for first place, $300 for second place, and $100 for third place.

There is no pair showing when the last card is dealt. Your hand is

and you are high on board and therefore must act first. Your last card is the

giving you aces full. You bet $1,000 in tournament chips.

The player on your immediate left has

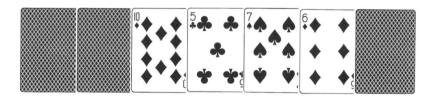

and is already all-in.

The next player calls with the last of his chips and has

The last of the four players, who has a huge stack, raises you $1,000. His hand is

Notice that he can beat your aces full only if his three down cards are all queens. Thus, you are an extremely heavy favorite, and in a ring game would reraise without hesitation. You have $1,100 remaining in your stack.

Would it be wise to raise with your last $100 in tournament chips and put yourself all-in? Probably not if the sharecropper method is being used. You will be risking $167 in real prize money for one tournament chip. The reason is that if the raiser does happen to have the "miracle" four queens, you will be eliminated from the tournament along with the other two players, and the three of you would receive $133 each.

$$\$133 = \frac{\$300 + \$100}{3}$$

However, if you merely call his raise and finish the hand with your last $100 chip, you will be virtually insuring yourself of sole possession of second place and the $300 that goes with it.

Therefore, although your aces full is an overwhelming favorite, it would be foolish to go all-in. One additional chip will not be a factor of any significance in a $1,000 limit heads-up confrontation.

Playing Short-Handed Poker

Generally speaking, when compared to the average home game player, most small stakes tournament players are, to varying degrees, competent players. However, due to the lack of experience in playing short-handed, many fail to properly adjust their playing requirements. For example, at a full hold 'em table, an

is usually unprofitable if you are the first player to act. However, if there are only two other players, the two blinds, you have a strong hand. As the number of players at your table declines, pay close attention to how the other players, especially the new faces in the tournament, are playing. It is usually safe to assume that a player who lacks experience at tournament poker will fail to properly adjust for a short-handed table.

This brings to mind an amusing personal experience. One day not long ago, while waiting for the start of a lowball tournament, I struck up a conversation with a young man I had never seen in the casino before. He was a nice, pleasant fellow who told me that he was in town for a few days to attend a sales convention and that he was familiar with the game of lowball because he had learned it from his dad. He went on to tell me that he still played the game occasionally as a substitute in his father's monthly dealer's choice games, but he had never before played in a poker tournament, and had no expectation of winning the tournament or even finishing in the money. As far as he was concerned, the thirteen-dollar buy-in was cheap enough for a "kick." Since this was a Progressive Stack Rebuy Tournament, being a nice fellow myself, I explained to the young man why rebuys were a good investment. In addition, I suggested that if he really wanted a "kick," he should be playing to win, and after all, another ten or twenty dollars was not really much of an investment. With a laugh, he agreed.

As luck would have it, we met again about three hours later as the last table was being formed. The young man thanked me for having talked him into making the rebuys and, with a chuckle, told me that he was going to leave the casino as a winner "no matter what."

We were still there when the tournament field was reduced to five players. Correctly assuming that the young man would fail to properly adjust for a short table, I then proceeded to shed my nice guy image and stole a few blinds from him. I knew that he would not know to call enough to stop me from taking more than my share.

For most percentage payback tournaments, the amount paid for first place is twice the amount paid for second place and four times the amount paid for third place. Because payment is so heavily skewed in favor of the higher finishers, it is vitally important for tournament players to master the art of playing short-handed poker. Strangely enough, as important as playing short-handed is for the tournament player, only a small amount appears in print. However, in their books, David Sklansky and Mason Malmuth have given us some helpful guidelines that I will briefly summarize for you.

First, Sklansky and Malmuth point out that short-handed play is really "very similar to being at a full table after several people have passed." Thus your opening and defending strategies should be about the same as if the first five or six (in the case of hold 'em) or the first four or five (in the case of stud) players have passed.

An important exception occurs in seven-card stud since the "total amount of the antes in the pot will not be as large as it is in an eight-handed game. Therefore, if the game is short-handed, you should steal less than you would in a full game."

For instance, suppose you were playing $15-$30 stud with a $2 ante and a $5 bring-in. If the game is eight-handed, the first five people pass, and now it is your turn and you decide to steal, you will be risking $15 to win $21.

Compare this to a three-handed stud game where you are first to act. In both cases there are two players left behind you, but instead of $21 to win there will now be only $11. So unless your opponents defend less, you should steal less often in this situation.

By the way, a $15-$30 limit game was used for this example because many players are familiar with games of that size. But this carries over no matter what the limit as long as there is an ante and a bring-in.

When playing hold 'em, Sklansky and Malmuth also point out that in order to stop someone from stealing too much on the flop, you need to make a lot of calls. In *Hold 'em Poker for Advanced Players,* they state "If you fold every time you don't have a pair, a draw, or overcards, then you are not calling (or raising) enough in a heads-up pot." For seven-card stud, they give similar advice in *Seven Card Stud for Advanced Players* (written with Ray Zee).

In addition to this advice, mastery of short-handed play will have to come from personal experience, tempered with sound judgment, and a good knowledge of your opponents. Also, as you gain this experience, keep in mind that the size of a player's stack will frequently dictate how he will play a marginal starting hand.

In any poker situation, one of the most important tools in a player's arsenal is the ability to correctly read other players at the table. This is especially important at the last table where the stakes are high and the players few. Watch the other players closely. You will usually find that most of the players will be playing quite conservatively because their primary objective at the moment is to move up the ladder or survive long enough to participate in a chop.

Pay close attention to which players are anxious to make a deal and which players are not. In most cases, players who are anxious to chop will be playing conservative, survival poker and will therefore be vulnerable to a bluff. The exception is the player whose earnest offer to chop has been rejected. Players who fall into this category sometimes go on tilt and come out charging. Invariably, such players are very inexperienced at tournament play and their lack of experience will be quite obvious.

In short-handed play, you will usually find yourself against one other player. Getting a correct read on your lone adversary in such a situation will often be critical to your chances. The first question that you need to ask yourself is a very simple one. How did he get involved in the hand? If he was forced to play the hand because he had the big blind or had to make a forced opening bet, it is usually safe to assume that he does not have much of a hand. However, if he has a comfortable stack and is playing the hand of his own volition, it would only be prudent to proceed with caution and give him credit for a good hand. Also, if your adversary is a solid tournament player who knows to "take advantage of tight play," you must be prepared to call him frequently in order to insure that an "automatic" steal attempt on his part is not immediately profitable.

Almost as important as watching other players is watching the clock. With huge blinds and betting limits, the timing of the next increase is sometimes more important than the skill of the players in determining final tournament placings. Be aware that some players will deliberately stall. Such action might force other players to go all-in because the blinds will now have doubled before it is their turn to take the blinds.

For example, if the player in the small blind is aware that the betting limits will increase in the next few seconds, he may pretend to be considering his next move when in fact he has no intention of doing anything except fold his hand. There is little that management can do to curb this kind of abuse, except limit the amount of time that the offending player will be allowed.

However, since such a limitation is cumbersome and all but impossible to administer on a timely basis, offenders are more than likely to be grudgingly tolerated. Another time when some players will put on this unethical stall is when the tournament field approaches the payoff point. For example, if all players who survive to the last two tables in a hold 'em tournament will share in the tournament pool, some players will start to stall when the field has declined to the low twenties. Tournament managers can curb this kind of abuse by having each of the last three tables play hand-to-hand when the field has declined to this number. In other words, in order to eliminate the incentive to stall, each of the last three tables will start their next hand simultaneously upon receipt of instructions from the tournament director.

The Collusion Stage

The great fear of many poker players is what is called "collusion" — that is the teaming up of some players, usually by secretly signaling the value of their hands to each other in order to give themselves an unfair advantage. Fortunately, collusion, as well as other forms of cheating, are very rare in public cardrooms. There are two reasons for this. First, cardroom management is well aware of the fact that this type of behavior is extremely bad for business. They therefore go to great lengths to insure that their games are clean. Second, the players themselves "police the game."

However, in the last stages of a poker tournament, there is a form of collusion between players that is not only legal, but frequently both ethical and proper strategy. Even in this situation, however, open discussion between players on how to best accomplish their mutual objective is forbidden. Instead, collusion takes place in more subtle forms such as flat calling where a raise might otherwise seem to be in order or automatically checking when another player is already all-in. The ability to promptly recognize such situations is vitally important to any tournament player who hopes to be successful.

The incentive to engage in this legalized form of collusion stems from the fact that payment to tournament finalists is so lopsidedly in favor of the top two places that minimizing another player's chances of surviving is sometimes more important than maximizing your chances of winning a hand. Notice that we have now reached that point where tournament play differs greatly from play in a standard ring game. In order to illustrate this point, assume that:

1. Players A, B, and C are the last three players remaining in a lowball draw tournament that will pay $1,000 for first place, $500 for second place, and $250 for third place;
2. Player A has the small blind and is all-in for $1,000;
3. Player B has the big blind for $2,000 and has a large stack;
4. Player C is in the dealer position with a large stack and is therefore the first player to act. He is holding

He has the best possible drawing hand in the game of lowball.

At an open table on the casino floor, Player C has a hand that any knowledgeable player would raise with. A raise would improve his chances of winning the hand by causing Player B to fold or make a bigger pot if Player B calls. However, in this tournament situation, Player C would be foolish to raise because if Player A is eliminated from the tournament, Player C's "guarantee" from the tournament would increase from $250 to $500. In other words, the most important consideration for Player C is not to win the hand but to minimize Player A's chance of survival. This Player C can do by simply calling the $2,000 blind and giving Player B a free draw. Notice that while it is true that Player B will occasionally get lucky and beat Player C, in this situation, the way for Player C to maximize his expectation is to play very differently than he would in an open game.

In the previous example, it was clear that the best strategy of action for Player C was to work in concert with Player B in order to eliminate Player A. However, in many instances, the proper course of action is not nearly as obvious. Consider for example the following scenario:

1. Players A, B, and C are among the last four players remaining in a lowball tournament that will pay $1,000 for first place, $500 for second place, $250 for third place, and $125 for fourth place;
2. Player A has the small blind and is all-in for $1,000;
3. Player B has the big blind for $2,000 and has only $1,000 left in his stack;
4. Player C is in the dealer position and has a huge stack. Once again, he has the best possible drawing hand of A♣2♦3♥JokerK♠;
5. Player D, the fourth player, also has a huge stack but has folded.

In this situation, it would probably be correct for Player C to raise. Although a raise might improve Player A's chances of surviving the hand (if Player B folds), it would put great pressure on Player B to call the raise because if he does surrender his $2,000 big blind, he will be severely crippled with only $1,000 remaining in his stack and the $1,000 small blind coming on the next hand. Another consideration is the fact that even if Player A does win the hand and survives, he can only win $3,000 in tournament chips and will therefore not pose an immediate threat to Player C. Thus, it would probably be in Player C's best interest to try to eliminate both Player A and Player B at the same time.

The two examples that were discussed above raise an important question for any tournament player. If you have a strong drawing hand late in a tournament, when is it best to cooperate with the other players in order to eliminate another player, and when is it advisable to raise, thereby possibly eliminating other potential callers? Although this may seem like a relatively simple question, it is in fact a complex, multifaceted question due to the numerous variables. However, in general, you should raise even though it might help another player survive if:

1. The player who you might be helping to survive will probably not pose an immediate threat to you even if he does win the hand;

2. There is a possibility that you might be able to eliminate more than one player;

3. There is a good possibility that you might be able to win a sizable pot.

Note that if this recommendation is followed, you will probably not be raising with a small or medium stack but would be considering a raise if you have a large stack. This is logical because a player with a small or medium stack should be primarily concerned about eliminating another player and moving one more step up the ladder. However, a player with a large stack who is in no immediate danger of being eliminated from the tournament should be primarily concerned with putting the most pressure on his opponents and adding to his stack, thus positioning himself to win the tournament. This strategy also allows him to profit from the fact that his penalty for losing the pot is not as great as his opponents penalty for losing the pot.

Finally, let me remind you again that if you are at the last table of a poker tournament with a large stack, you must avoid getting into a raising war with another player who also has a large stack until you are virtually certain that you are holding the winning hand. (This idea is particularly important at the end of a tournament when only a few players are left.)

The Most
Beatable Tournaments

I won't tell you my age, but I've been spending time at the poker tables for more than fifty years. During the forties, I played in shacks that served as quarters for high school students who were helping out on summer harvests. During the fifties, I played in college dormitories and also aboard a variety of ships at sea. During the sixties, seventies, and eighties, I played on military installations in overseas areas, and now during the nineties, I am playing in casinos.

During these fifty years, I have played poker with many thousands of people. Since I have never once played with someone who did not enjoy winning, I will assume that you too enjoy winning. This raises an interesting question. At what kind of tournament are you most likely to be a winner?

Now that is a very simple question, and my guess is that you have never once stopped to ask it. You are not alone. The vast majority of players probably haven't considered this. I have been playing in poker tournaments for more than ten years, but didn't get around to asking myself this question until about a month before this writing The idea came to me while driving home from a losing effort in a lowball tournament.

The good news is that the answer to this question is also very simple: The easiest tournament to beat is the one in which the game being offered is not usually played in the sponsoring casino. For example, if seven-card stud high-low split eight-or-better is not normally spread for small-stakes players, but the casino does sponsor a seven-card stud high-low split eight-or-better tournament, that will be the easiest tournament to beat. If the game is not spread in the casino, the likelihood is strong that the regular players will not be familiar with it and will therefore play it poorly. For instance, in a local seven-card stud high-low split eight-or-better tournament, some of the players will be so unfamiliar with the game that they fail to recognize a situation in which they have a lock on the low half of the pot and have a chance to scoop the whole pot if they make a straight or a flush. I see far fewer mistakes of this kind in games such as hold 'em and seven-card stud (high), which are widely played in the casinos.

In my case, the most beatable tournaments are the lowball tournaments. When I find that I can no longer win in a lowball game where some players are routinely raising from an early position with a two-card draw and betting very rough pat hands into my one-card draws, I will know that it is definitely time to consider packing up and heading back to the farm. By the way, if you play lowball in the manner that I have just described, don't expect to do very well in any tournament or ring game.

Another factor to be considered in finding the most beatable tournament is the time of the month, especially for weekday tournaments that are played during the morning or early afternoon hours. Many small tournament regulars are social security recipients or other retirees who are on tight budgets and therefore do not have adequate funds to make unlimited rebuys at the end of the month. This could be an important factor, especially for progressive stack rebuy events.

Now that we have determined which tournaments are the *most* beatable, how do we go about acquiring the skills needed to beat them if the game is not being played in the local casino? Once again, the answer is really quite simple: Go out and buy yourself a good book.

Merely reading the book, and maybe even giving it some thought will not make you an expert, but it will give you a decided edge over most of the other players in the tournament because, trust me, most small-stakes tournament players are notorious non-readers. On occasion, you may find one of them reading the *Racing Form* or *Card Player Magazine,* but you won't find too many articles about a seldom played game such as lowball or seven-card stud high-low split eight-or-better?

I have read numerous books on poker and poker strategy. Some of these books are excellent. Others are, to be very diplomatic, considerably less than excellent. For the small-stakes player who is interested in learning how to beat one of these most beatable tournaments, I recommend:

1. For high-low split games: *High-Low Split Poker for Advanced Players* by Ray Zee. This book should be especially helpful for those who are interested in playing seven-card stud high-low split eight-or-better, which seems to be increasing in popularity as a tournament event much more rapidly than as a regular game on the casino floor. The reason is probably because casino management does not look with favor on high-low split games because of the simple fact that such games require that pots be split between the high hand and the low hand. Obviously, the more hands that are played, the more frequently the casino will be able to rake the pot, and the splitting of pots takes time.

2. For lowball: *Winning Concepts in Draw and Lowball* by Mason Malmuth. Although much of this book is devoted to draw poker, which is now rarely played in casinos, this book contains the best and most comprehensive coverage of lowball that is currently in print.

See Appendix B at the end of this book for other recommended reading.

Part Eight

Stepping Up

Stepping Up

Introduction

The Tournament Trail section of a recent issue of *Card Player Magazine* listed 497 small-stakes poker tournaments that are being conducted in this country each week. Therefore, when you consider that there are numerous tournaments that are not even being reported, it is probably safe to assume that close to 30,000 small-stakes poker tournaments occur each year. In contrast, there are only a relatively small number of major events, even though some of these events consist of many tournaments.

These figures are provided not because I wish to downplay the significance of major tournaments, but to put the numbers into proper perspective and point out that the number of small-stakes tournament players greatly exceeds the number of those who play in major tournaments. Obviously, however, the majors are where the money, fame, and glory are to be found. Consequently, many small-stakes players will, from time to time, attempt to make the transition to tournaments at a higher level. This chapter is intended to provide such players insight into the larger tournaments and, hopefully, help them make the adjustments that will be necessary to successfully compete at the higher level.

The term "major tournament" is an extremely broad and ambiguous one that has never been satisfactorily defined. For our purposes, however, a major tournament is any tournament that is listed as a major tournament in the Tournament Trail of *Card Player Magazine*. This means that the buy-in could range from as low as $115 to as high as $25,000.

The most popular buy-in for major tournaments is currently in the range of $330 to $540. However, with the increasing popularity of tournament poker, buy-ins of $120 to $230 seem to be increasing. For example, the $120 buy-in limit hold 'em tournament at the 1997 Orleans Open in Las Vegas drew a phenomenal 912 entrants.

In general, the initial stack for a tournament with a buy-in of less than $500 (not including the service charge) is $500 in tournament chips. For tournaments with buy-ins that exceed $500, the initial stack is usually the amount of the buy-in, minus the service charge. In other words, the initial stack for a tournament that costs $1,050 to enter will be $1,000, and the initial stack for a tournament that costs $1,580 to enter will be $1,500.

Major tournaments generally fall into one of two broad categories: They are either No Rebuy Tournaments or Constant Stack Rebuy Tournaments. A few years ago, the shootout format was used for some major tournaments. However, these types of events are now rarely seen. To the best of my knowledge, the Progressive Stack Rebuy Format and the Sudden Sayonara Format have never been used for a major tournament.

Aside from the obvious fact that the stakes are usually much higher, most major tournaments differ significantly from the small-stakes tournaments discussed in Parts Two and Three of this book in only the following respects:

1. Betting limits in major tournaments are raised much more slowly than in small stakes tournaments. In general, for the less expensive major tournaments, betting limits are raised at forty minute intervals. For the more expensive tournaments, a one-hour interval is the norm. This compares with intervals of fifteen and twenty minutes for most small-stakes tournaments.

2. The caliber of the average player in major tournaments is higher than in most small-stakes tournaments. There are a few small-stakes tournament players who seem to enjoy harboring the notion that the primary difference is that major tournament players have more money. In my personal

experience, anybody who truly believes this will be proved very wrong. Take my word for it: At any level of poker, be it a tournament or an open table, the higher the stakes, the higher the caliber of play. There are very few exceptions.

No Rebuy
Major Tournaments

Limit Games

Since the vast majority of major tournaments are no rebuy limit tournaments, we will begin with a discussion of them. For this purpose, let's assume that the initial stack is $500 in tournament chips and the following betting limits are applicable:

Betting Limits	
First level	$15-$30
Second level	$30-$60
Third level	$50-$100
Fourth level	$100-$200
Fifth level	$150-$300
Sixth level	$300-$600
Seventh level	$500-$1,000
Eight level	$1,000-$2,000
Ninth level	$2,000-$4,000

For most major tournaments, the initial stack is $500 and the opening betting limits are $15 and $30. Therefore, even for those tournaments in which limits were increased after forty minutes of play, betting limits have only doubled to $30 and $60 after an hour. However, because opening limits are relatively large in relation to the size of the initial stack, opening action in a major tournament is usually much more conservative than in a small-stakes tournament. This contributes to a slower pace of action.

131

The First Three Levels

In general, during the first stages of play, you can expect to find the following four categories of players in a major tournament:

1. **Type A players: The experienced and technically sound who can be expected to start off conservatively.** When encountering these players, you can expect them to bet their hand for value, press any advantage that they might have, and attempt to steal the pot if the opportunity presents itself. Do not expect a Type A player to be playing with a mediocre starting hand unless he or she happened to have had one of the blinds, had the forced bring-in, or were on a very short stack. The majority of players will fall into this category.

2. **Type B players: The experienced and technically sound who can be expected to start off fast.** Unlike the Type A player who will usually begin play fairly conservatively, the Type B will attempt to quickly acquire a large stack due to the advantages this will give him later in the tournament. In other words, these are solid players who are willing to risk "bombing out" in order to try to get an early lead over their rivals.

3. **Type C players: The weak players.** This category includes small-stakes tournament players who are trying to move up, occasional major tournament players, and tourists who "just happened to be in town." As a rule, Type C players have little chance among a field of professionals. However, these players do occasionally manage to make a few key hands and

go all the way. Type C players are rarely found in tournaments that have buy-ins in excess of $500.[6]

4. **Type D players: The Kamikazes.** These are the players who take playing fast to an extreme. They are likely to be betting and raising on almost any hand. A few years ago, it was not uncommon to find a significant number of Type D players in a major tournament. However, over the years, the number of Type D players entering major tournaments seems to have diminished considerably. The probable reason is that Type D players have virtually no chance in a field of solid, high-caliber players, and it doesn't take them forever to figure that out for themselves.

Many players who are stepping up to a higher level have a tendency to be somewhat intimidated by the competition. Don't let that happen to you. In any poker tournament, short-term luck always plays a large role. Therefore, enter the tournament with the attitude that you are a competent player who, with a little luck, is capable of winning it all.

In major tournaments, because three or four rounds will be played at each level, you will have time to settle in and get a feel for your table. Like the Type A player described above, play your best solid, relatively conservative poker. However, if you feel that you have the best of it during the course of a hand, tend to be aggressive and try to get maximum return. Survival is always an important consideration in a tournament. However, if you feel that you have an opportunity to build a stack, don't be afraid to gamble a bit in order to achieve this, especially in the early going.

Many players who enter a major tournament are professionals who travel the circuit. Others will be local professionals who play

---

[6] An exception to this is the $10,000 no-limit hold 'em championship at the World Series of Poker where many small stakes players qualify via satellites on Internet poker sites.

in a large number of local tournaments. A few will be top-side game players who are highly skilled at the particular form of poker they are participating in. For the most part, these players are familiar faces. If you are seen as an inexperienced tournament player or a small-stakes tournament player who is stepping up in class for this tournament, be aware that some of your opponents, especially the Type B players, may try to intimidate you. Therefore, if you suspect that this may be the case, be inclined to stand your ground. In this regard, keep in mind that, in general, players in a major tournament tend to be more predictable than the average player in a small-stakes tournament. That's because they will probably not be routinely playing weak starting hands. For example, assume that you are in big blind and the pot was not raised before the flop. You have

The flop comes

In a major tournament, the cards shown above are not likely to have helped any of the other players. It is highly possible that you are holding the best hand at this point in time. In a small stakes tournament, I would be far less inclined to make such a judgment.

The Fourth, Fifth, and Sixth Levels

By the end of the third level of play, you can usually expect that approximately one-third to one-half of the players will have been eliminated.

When considering that the initial stack was only $500 in tournament chips and betting limits at the start of the fourth level are $100 and $200, it is inevitable that the casualty list will begin to mount much more rapidly. However, since you still must outlast two-thirds of the original tournament field, it is much too early to go into the survival mode. If you feel that you have the upper hand, aggressively press your advantage and don't be shy about putting in a raise or two if you believe that such action might improve your chances of winning the hand. However, as in any poker situation, there is always room for sound judgment. For example, when playing hold 'em if you raised with

got several callers and the flop comes

you should probably fold if there is action.

The End Game

Depending on the size of the tournament field, the end game will usually begin during the seventh or eight level of play. Since the size of the tournament pool has little bearing on the strategy for the end game, your attention is directed to "The End Game" (on pages 60-62 in Part Two of this book).

No-Limit and Pot-limit Games

No-limit No Rebuy Tournaments are usually the featured event for casinos that sponsor major tournaments. However, because the buy-in for these tournaments is usually very high and the number of players who are experienced in no-limit play is relatively small, these tournaments normally attract an elite few. My discussion of these tournaments will therefore be limited to a few brief comments.

Many of these tournaments, especially those with the highest buy-ins, extend over two days. The $10,000 buy-in main event of the World Series of Poker extends over five days, for example.

Early action in most major no-limit tournaments tend to be extremely slow. There are two reasons for this. First, the opening blinds are usually very small in relation to the size of the initial stack. Therefore, there is a tendency to give early raisers credit and not challenge them because the other players do not have much of a stake in the pot at the time of the raise. Second, many players open play very cautiously because they are reluctant to risk being one of the first casualties. Apparently, they feel that there is a stigma to being knocked out early. This will usually not deter the Type B player.

Major no-limit tournaments are not for the novice. If you intend to play in one of these tournaments, it is strongly recommended that you begin with a satellite. This will give you valuable experience as well as a feel for the type of action that you can expect to encounter.

Another thing to keep in mind is that the major no-limit tournaments start off favoring those players with real poker skill as opposed to tournament skill. There are three reasons for this.

A. The initial stack is larger relative to the size of the starting blinds.

B. The limits — which in this case means the size of the blinds — are increased more slowly. Thus, you will have more time to use sophisticated poker skills.

C. In no-limit the edge that the good player has over the bad player is greater. This is not a function of the tournament, but a function of the game itself. This allows the best no-limit players to dominate these events in a manner that the best limit players are unable to achieve in the limit tournaments.

What can you conclude from this? Simply that until you get some experience at no-limit poker and/or no-limit tournaments, entering them can be very dangerous for your bankroll. They may be fun to play, but don't expect to do very well at first.

Similar comments apply to pot-limit events as well, even though the playing strategy for pot-limit is sometimes very different than no-limit.

Constant Stack Rebuy Major Tournaments

Limit Games

In major tournaments in which limit poker is played, rebuys are usually permitted only until the first intermission. In general, only one rebuy is permitted, but a few tournaments allow two rebuys. Although unlimited rebuys are allowed in some no-limit and pot-limit tournaments, it is rare to find a limit tournament in which more that two rebuys are allowed.

As the tournament begins, it is useful to know which players at your table are planning to make a rebuy and which are not. This will probably give you a clue as to how they will be playing. As a rule, players who plan to rebuy will be playing more aggressively than players who do not plan to rebuy. Before play begins, try to get this information from the players at your table. You may be surprised at how readily some of them will give you such useful information. However, never divulge your own true intentions.

Remember, in a percentage payback tournament, a solid player will almost always have a positive expectation when he makes a rebuy. Therefore, you should assume that the professionals at your table will be making a rebuy if they lose their stack or get low on chips. You should do the same.

A few years ago it was not uncommon to find many players entering these major tournaments who had little understanding of correct tournament strategy and who also were mediocre as poker players. With the rapid expansion of casinos across the country, and the proliferation of poker tournaments, those days are now long gone. However, there are still exceptions, especially in the tournaments that have buy-ins of less than $500. Play close attention to the type of hands that players at your table are playing. Since there will be three or four rounds at the first betting level, it should be possible to get a reasonably good read of your current opponents.

The Rebuy Period

In most rebuy tournaments, players who plan to make a rebuy will be playing fast while players who do not plan to rebuy will be playing a more conservative style of poker. Playing fast is good strategy if you plan to rebuy because it will maximize your chances of building a stack while leaving you the rebuy option.

If you can't rebuy, my advice is not to play the tournament. You will be at a disadvantage to those good tournament players who intend to rebuy if necessary.

However, if you do enter the tournament and can't rebuy, I recommend that you still play aggressively. It is my experience that most players who do not plan to rebuy play much too conservatively. The reason that I still recommend aggressive play is that with only $500 in chips and a large field, prospects for surviving to the payoff point are slim. Therefore, I believe that your long-term prospects should be maximized by being aggressive. In other words, don't be afraid to "bomb out" early. If you are to win this tournament (or any other tournament for that matter) you must get lucky and you are more likely to get lucky when you play aggressively since this style of play tends to produce more playing errors from your opponents. (They give you free cards, they miss bets, they try to slowplay too often against you, they steal too little, and so forth.)

The Intermediate Stage

As was indicated earlier, the intermediate stage extends from the end of the rebuy period to that point at which players begin to be concerned about the number of players remaining in the tournament.

With the end of the rebuy period, the pace of the action usually slows noticeably, at least for a few minutes. Be sure that you take advantage of the tight play that results whenever the opportunity presents itself and do not be afraid to try a steal. Otherwise, play solid, patient poker.

Because of the rebuys that have been made, the casualty list will usually not begin to mount significantly until late in the first level after the intermission. With the start of the second level of play, the casualty list will grow rapidly and many players will be closely watching the clock and the position of the blinds. Be sure that you do likewise.

The End Game

Much of the advice here is still the same as before. See "The End game" on pages 75-77 in Part Three of this book.

No-Limit and Pot-Limit Games

Because of the high cost of the buy-in for most no-limit tournaments and the relatively small number of players who are proficient at no-limit poker, these tournaments usually attract only the elite few. An exception is the world championship event at the World Series of Poker, which now attracts as many as 1,000 or more entrants in spite of the $10,000 buy-in. That tournament is, however, a no rebuy event.

The buy-in for most of these no-limit rebuy tournaments range from $540 to $5,080. Since many of these events allow unlimited rebuys, they are definitely not intended for the novice. As with the No Rebuy No-Limit Tournaments, if you plan to enter one of these tournaments for the first time, it is recommended that you begin with a satellite.

These comments also apply to some of the pot-limit rebuy events. They are not for the novice and can prove to be very expensive if you are forced to make many rebuys. This is especially true for pot-limit Omaha.

.

Part Nine

Tips for
Tournament Managers

Tips for
Tournament Managers

Introduction

I find tournaments to be not only profitable, but a lot of fun to play. I believe most casino managers feel the same way. Tournaments are good for business and help to create a feeling of "good times" in a cardroom. But, like many endeavors, they could use a little improvement.

What follows are some suggestions that should make tournaments run a little more smoothly, and thus return more to the players and the hosting casino. If these ideas are adopted, everyone should benefit.

Recommendations

Tournament managers, take note: The small-stakes in-house poker tournament as well as a major tournament is a promotional tool for your casino. Obviously, the more enjoyable the tournament is for your players, the more successful it will be in this area and the more players you will be able to attract for future events.

By putting the following recommendations into action the result will be better managed, more player-friendly tournaments in your casino.

1. **Give players who sign up for the tournament early an option in the selecting of a seat at the first table.** Many small tournament regulars are elderly retirees who have difficulty seeing the cards from certain seats. This problem can be largely resolved while still maintaining the randomness of seat selection by using two bowls for seating chits. For example, if it is known that there will be at least five tables for a game that will have nine players at a table, put chits for seat numbers 1,4,5,6, and 9 for the first five tables in one of the bowls, and all of the other chits in the second bowl. Until all of the chits in the first bowl are taken, allow players the option to draw a chit from the bowl of their choice. In addition to providing an improved service for retirees who form the core of many small-stakes tournaments, this policy will encourage some of the players to sign up for the tournament early.

2. **Always start the tournament at the scheduled time.** Many small-stakes tournaments and some large ones as well do not start until long after the advertised starting time. Not only is this an unnecessary irritant for players who have already

signed up and are therefore subjected to a long wait, it is an extremely poor business practice. The purpose of the tournament is to bring players into the casino with the hope that they will later play at an open table on the casino floor. Obviously, tournament players will not be available to play at an open table if they are still seated in the tournament.

It is my experience that players will quickly adapt to the starting time of a tournament as long as the tournament director consistently adheres to that starting time. The result will be more orderly and better managed events that will be a more effective and enjoyable promotional tool.

3. **Kill the hand if the player is not at the table to act on the hand.** In his turn, a player is obligated to act on his hand by betting, calling, checking, raising, or folding. Since no other player is permitted to act on his hand, if a player is not in his seat, the hand should be immediately killed by the dealer. This will minimize confusion and speed up play.

4. **When moving a player in a game that is played with blinds, move the player who is in the same position relative to the blinds.** When necessary to move a player from one table to another in order to balance out the number of players at the tables, it is customary to draw cards, with the player who drew the largest card (or the lowest card for lowball) moving to the short table. This sometimes results in gross inequities. A player who has just had the blinds might be moved to a table where he would again be required to post the blinds, or a player who just played a full round gets to play another full round without posting any blinds. This problem can be largely resolved by moving the player who is in the same seat relative to the dealer button.

5. **If a player who has prepaid the entry fee does not arrive by the end of the first intermission, pick up his chips.** The

presence of a "dead" hand because of an absent player needlessly distorts play. For example, if you are the small blind and the dead hand is to your left with the big blind, the fact that the other players know that the big blind will not call will make you more vulnerable to a raise. The same is true in seven-card stud. The presence of the dead hand to your left will cause the same problem when that (absent) player has the forced bring-in.

Prior to the intermission, the betting limits are relatively small. However, after the intermission, the presence of a few chips at an empty seat should not be allowed to distort play. It should be clear that the absent player is not going to show.

Another factor to be considered is that players at a table with an absent player are at an advantage in a tournament with only a small number of players because survival strategies play such an important role. Clearly, it will be much easier to outlast your opponents if they are not all present.

6. **When consolidating tables near the end of a tournament, allow a player who has just taken the blinds to select a seat that will not require that he again take the big blind on his first hand at his new table.** The current practice when tables are consolidated near the end of a tournament is all remaining players draw for seats. As a result, it is possible for a player who just had the blinds to be forced into taking the big blind on his first hand at his new table. This is extremely unfair and needlessly adds to the crap shoot nature of poker tournaments.

It is my opinion, and I believe that the vast majority of tournament players will agree with me, that pure luck that has nothing to do with the playing of poker should be minimized as a factor in determining where a player finishes in a poker tournament. Therefore, I suggest that the following simple but imminently more equitable method be used.

A. When consolidating two tables into one table, the two players who would have had the big blind on the next hand and the two players to their immediate left would draw from cards marked 2,3,4 and 5. They then would take seats that correspond to those numbers at the last table. All other remaining players would draw from cards marked 1,6,7, etc. and take seats accordingly.

B. When consolidating from three tables to two, the three players who would have had the big blind on the next hand, and the three players to their immediate left, would draw from cards marked as follows and take corresponding seats at tables that have been designated as spades and hearts.

Spades: 2,3, and 4
Hearts: 2,3, and 4

All other remaining players would draw for seats from spades and hearts marked 1,5,6,7, etc.

7. **When selling add-on stacks, make only one trip to each table.** The add-on option is usually a bargain because the cost of a chip has been reduced to its lowest level. As a result, confusion and arguments may result. For example, assume that each player has an option to make an add-on ($500 in tournament chips for $10) or a double add-on ($1,000 in chips for $20). Suppose a player has already made an add-on using his last $10. However, after the chip seller has left the table, a friend offers to give him an additional $10, and he wishes to purchase an additional $500 in tournament chips. Unfortunately, another player objects because he believes that this person has already purchased the maximum number of chips that are allowed, and the chip seller does not remember how many chips he sold to him.

Disputes of this type can be avoided by establishing a simple policy. Once the chip seller leaves a table, no additional chips will be sold at that table. *Absolutely no exceptions.*

8. **If a payout is computed at $600 or only slightly more than $600, make the payout $599.** If a player is paid $600 or more from a tournament, the casino is required to issue the player IRS Form W-2G. In such a situation, the overwhelming majority of players would prefer to receive the lesser amount.

9. **When making payments to tournament finalists, use casino chips rather than cash currency.** Use of casino chips is preferable to cash currency for the following reasons:

   A. When cash currency is used, amounts to be paid must be counted out bill by bill whereas with casino chips, the amounts are much more readily discernible. As a result, with casino chips, the process is not only faster but is accomplished in a smoother, more professional manner.

   B. The primary purpose of the small-stakes, in-house tournament is to encourage activity within the casino. It is a psychological fact of life that a person in your casino with a pocket full of chips is more likely to part with some of his money than the person who has his pockets full of greenbacks.

   C. For the same reason as B above, the use of casino chips is more likely to result in tokes for the dealers. This is a factor that should be very important. At many of the small-stakes tournaments, the amounts that are being left as tokes can be best described as pathetic, and this change should help to alleviate this problem.

Part Ten

Questions and Answers

Questions and Answers

Introduction

We have covered a great deal of material in this book. However, for many people, reading and learning can be two different things. Consequently, to help you retain some of the more significant ideas, we have reiterated them in a question-and-answer format.

I suggest that after you have read and studied the text, you try to answer the following questions. You probably will want to go over them many times. In addition, you should cover the answer that immediately follows each question. Only look at the solution after you have answered the question to the best of your ability.

Also, what follows is not a substitute for the text. In fact, some of the ideas in the text are not contained here. But enough material is included so that after you have thoroughly digested the text, the questions should help keep your tournament game sharp.

Finally, the questions and answers are organized by topics covered in the text, so you can easily return to the appropriate section for a full explanation.

Progressive Stack Rebuy Tournaments

The First Twenty Minutes

1. Should you play extremely loose during the rebuy period?
   No.

2. How should you play if you are in danger of being forced to make a rebuy?
   Play solid, conservative poker.

3. What if you have a larger stack than your adversary?
   Be aggressive and try to force him to make a rebuy.

4. Should you be playing fast?
   No.

5. Why?
   Fast play is likely to put you in a position where you might be forced to make an early rebuy while tournament chips are still being sold at a premium price.

6. Why is a small chip lead in the early minutes important?
   It will often determine who will be making the early rebuys.

7. When should you discard a good hand?
   When you are very low on chips and the rebuy stack will soon increase.

8. If the tournament is no-limit, should you make an all-in call with a mediocre starting hand?

No.

9. How should you be playing (in a no-limit tournament)?

Aggressively when appropriate, especially if you have a larger stack than your adversary and/or believe that you have the best of it going in.

The Second Twenty Minutes

1. How should you play during the second twenty minutes?

Essentially the same as the first twenty minutes.

2. What if you are on a short stack?

You may liberalize your play somewhat.

3. What else should you be prepared to do?

Take advantage of the loose play of some players who may be playing recklessly in an effort to catch up.

The Third Twenty Minutes

1. How should you be playing?

There is little need to consider tournament strategy as opposed to poker strategy.

2. When should you make a rebuy?

Whenever you are eligible to do so.

3. What if you don't intend to rebuy?

You will be putting yourself at a disadvantage to those players who rebuy correctly.

4. How much should you play down your stack to make a rebuy?
A good rule of thumb is one big bet.

5. What if you are on a small stack?
Continue to play solid, sensible poker and make an add-on at the intermission.

6. Why?
You will have little to gain unless you get a call (or a raise) and now you will probably be up against a superior hand.

The Intermediate Stage

1. When does the intermediate stage end?
Usually when the number of players remaining is approximately one full table more than the number who finish in the money.

2. What is the characteristic of the intermediate stage?
The pace of the action usually slows.

3. What should you do?
Take advantage of this tight play, particularly if you are up against a short stack or you are the first one excluding the blinds to enter the pot. Otherwise, play solid poker.

The End Game

1. What do most of the players who have small stacks do?
They begin to play conservatively.

2. Suppose you have a large stack. What should your strategy be?
Concentrate on eliminating players who have small stacks.

3. What if another player with a large stack bets into you?
   Do not get into a raising war unless you are virtually certain you have the best hand.

4. Suppose you have a medium stack. What should your strategy be?
   Avoid confrontations with players who have large stacks unless you feel you have a clear advantage, and concentrate on the smaller stacks.

5. If you play a hand, what should you do?
   Play it aggressively, but if the hand goes bad and you can save a few chips, you should always do so.

6. Suppose you have a small stack. What should your strategy be?
   Pay attention to the location of the dealer button and the stacks of the players who will be required to post before you do, and adjust accordingly.

7. What if you do decide to play a hand?
   Do so aggressively, but if the hand goes bad and you can save even one chip, do so.

8. If a blind is coming up soon on a player with a small stack what must you be prepared to do?
   Stand your ground if you have a reasonable number of chips.

9. What if the player with the small stack has several hands to go before he is required to put up a blind?
   Give him credit for a good hand.

10.What is important when you are in late position?
   The chip status of the two blinds.

11. What must you be aware of?

    Your raise might force a player in the blind to call.

12. Suppose the players in the blinds are not calling enough and your hand does have legitimate value?

    This is an excellent opportunity to take advantage of tight play.

No Rebuy Tournaments

The First Twenty Minutes

1. What do you usually see?
   Extremely loose play in the opening stages.

2. Should you play this way?
   No.

3. What should you do?
   Try to take advantage of opponents who play too many hands and go too far with their hands.

4. Examples?
   In hold 'em, liberally play small pairs, medium-suited connectors, and ace-little suited. In stud, liberally play small pairs (particularly if they are buried), small three flushes, and three cards to a straight with a gap, especially if you can get in for only the bring-in and your cards are live.

5. What else should you be willing to do?
   Use the check-raise more liberally, especially if you are in early position.

6. What if you hold a monster?
   If you are in late position be inclined to slowplay providing the pot is not too big. Otherwise bet.

7. What should be your objective early in the tournament?
   To build your stack.

8. What about late in the tournament?
   Now you want to knock other players out.

The Second Twenty Minutes

1. What will begin to happen?
   The field will begin to thin.

2. What if you have been playing as recommended?
   There should be no immediate threat.

3. What should you be aware of?
   Many players will be forced to defend the blinds with hands they might otherwise abandon.

4. What does this mean?
   It might not be correct strategy to try to steal with some hands that you normally would.

5. What else should you look for?
   Players who have entered the tournament with the attitude that they will just "give it a shot." They will be difficult to bluff.

The End Game

1. When will the end game begin?
   Almost immediately after the intermission.

2. Suppose you have a large stack. What should your strategy be?
   Concentrate on eliminating players who have small stacks.

3. What if another player with a large stack bets into you?
   Do not get into a raising war unless you are virtually certain you have the best hand.

4. Suppose you have a medium stack. What should your strategy be?
   Avoid confrontations with players who have large stacks unless you feel you have a clear advantage, and concentrate on the smaller stacks.

5. If you play a hand, what should you do?
   Play it aggressively, but if the hand goes bad and you can save a few chips, you should always do so.

6. Suppose you have a small stack. What should your strategy be?
   Pay attention to the location of the dealer button and the stacks of players who will be required to post before you do, and adjust accordingly.

7. What if you do decide to play a hand?
   Do so aggressively, but if the hand goes bad and you can save even one chip, do so.

8. If a blind is coming up soon on a player with a small stack what must you be prepared to do?
   Stand your ground if you have a reasonable number of chips.

9. What if the player with the small stack has several hands to go before he is required to put up a blind?
   Give him credit for a good hand.

10. What is important when you are in late position?
    The chip status of the two blinds.

11. What must you be aware of?
    Your raise might force a player in the blind to call.

12. Suppose the players in the blinds are not calling enough and your hand does have legitimate value?
    This is an excellent opportunity to take advantage of tight play.

Constant Stack Rebuy Tournaments

The First Thirty Minutes

1. What is the play generally like?

    It is more conservative than either progressive stack rebuy tournaments or no rebuy tournaments.

2. Why?

    The rebuy is generally more expensive than the progressive stack rebuy tournament and the initial stack is smaller than the no rebuy tournament.

3. How does the play compare to games on the casino floor?

    The early action is generally more aggressive.

4. What is the recommended strategy?

    Play solid but be prepared to take advantage of loose play.

5. When should you make a rebuy?

    Whenever you are low on chips.

6. Should you play fast if you intend to rebuy?

    Even though it is theoretically correct, if the play is very loose (as it is in some small-stakes tournaments) you should slow down and make the appropriate adjustments for loose play.

The Second Thirty Minutes

1. How should you play against players who do not plan to rebuy and are forced to commit?
    Try to take advantage of them. Consider a raise in order to isolate a player with a short stack.

2. What if you have a large stack?
    Your expectation for an add-on may be negative.

3. In practice will this happen very often?
    No, except in a no-limit tournament.

4. What should you do if you have a lot of chips and are considering an add-on?
    Check the stacks of the other players.

5. What if the sponsoring casino is adding significant funds to the tournament pool?
    Exercise all rebuy and add-on options.

The Intermediate Stage

1. When does the intermediate stage typically end?
    Fifteen to thirty minutes after the end of the rebuy period.

2. What usually happens to the action following the end of the rebuy period?
    It slows down.

3. If a lot of players are playing survival poker, what should you do?
    Take advantage of tight play by being more aggressive.

4. When is this approach optimal?
   When you are in late position and/or are against players with short stacks.

The End Game

1. Suppose you have a large stack. What should your strategy be?
   Concentrate on eliminating players who have small stacks.

2. What if another player with a large stack bets into you?
   Do not get into a raising war unless you are virtually certain you have the best hand.

3. Suppose you have a medium stack. What should your strategy be?
   Avoid confrontations with players who have large stacks unless you feel you have a clear advantage, and concentrate on the smaller stacks.

4. If you play a hand, what should you do?
   Play it aggressively, but if the hand goes bad and you can save a few chips, you should always do so.

5. Suppose you have a small stack. What should your strategy be?
   Pay attention to the location of the dealer button and the stacks of players who will be required to post before you do, and adjust accordingly.

6. What if you do decide to play a hand?
   Do so aggressively, but if the hand goes bad and you can save even one chip, do so.

7. If a blind is coming up soon on a player with a small stack what must you be prepared to do?
   Stand your ground if you have a reasonable number of chips.

8. What if the player with the small stack has several hands to go before he is required to put up a blind?

> Give him credit for a good hand.

9. What is important when you are in late position?

> The chip status of the two blinds.

10. What must you be aware of?

> Your raise might force a player in the blind to call.

11. Suppose the players in the blinds are not calling enough and your hand does have legitimate value?

> This is an excellent opportunity to take advantage of tight play.

Sudden Sayonara Tournaments

Overview

1. What is the predetermined percentage method?
   A method of payment in which the amounts to be paid to the final players are determined in advance as a percentage of the total amount of money in the tournament pool.

2. What is the chip count ratio method?
   A method of payment in which the amounts to be paid to the final players are based on the percentage of the total chips that each player has after the last hand.

Strategy

1. What is a critical factor in determining correct strategy for the last few hands of the tournament?
   The method of payment that will be used.

2. If the predetermined percentage method is used what must you be aware of?
   Situations arise when it is correct to fold an extremely strong hand or call with a very weak hand.

3. What do you need to be kept informed of at the end of the tournament if the predetermined percentage is used?
   The chip position of the other players.

Shootout Tournaments

The First Table

1. Why is the strategy simple?
   There is no need to consider such factors as rebuy or survival strategy.

2. What should you be cognizant of in the opening minutes of play?
   That the betting limits will be increasing very rapidly.

3. How should you play any hands that you play?
   Aggressively.

4. What does this mean?
   Bet your hand for value and press any advantage that you think you have.

5. What is the real key to success at the first table?
   The ability to make proper adjustments as the number of players at your table declines.

6. Why is survival not a consideration?
   There will only be one winner at your table, which means that the chips do not change value.

The Second Session

1. What skill is key?
   Playing short-handed.

2. What is unique about the second session?
   It is the only situation in tournament play where players will all have stacks of equal size late in a tournament.

3. What does this mean?
   The previous recommendations on how to play different size stacks do not apply.

4. How do players who refuse a chop usually play?
   They tend to be aggressive.

5. What about the players in favor of making a deal?
   They typically will open play cautiously and try to move up the ladder.

6. What is an exception?
   The player who might have gone on tilt because his offer to chop was rejected.

7. What tendency frequently exists among players who favor making a deal?
   They try to "get" the renegade.

Last Table Negotiations

The Amount at Stake

1. Is the total amount of money at stake the total remaining in the tournament pool?
   No, it is always some fraction of that amount.

2. Why?
   Because each remaining player is guaranteed the payout of the lowest place that he can finish.

3. What does this mean?
   It means that the value of a chip in a large stack is lower than the value of a chip in a small stack.

4. What else do you need to consider if you are one of the players with a small stack?
   Whether a player with a large stack is an optimist or a pessimist.

5. What is the pessimist more likely to do?
   Agree to an offer that concedes him first place.

6. When does the standard chopping formula work well?
   If the stacks of the last few players are reasonably equal in size.

7. What if the stacks are much different?
   The standard formula overpays the large stacks.

8. What is the usual practice in these cases?
   For the players with a large stack to pay players with a small stack a premium.

The Position of the Dealer Button

1. For which games is the dealer button important?
   Omaha, hold 'em, and lowball.

2. Who does it affect most?
   Players who advance to the last table with a short stack.

3. Why is having good position with a short stack so important?
   It gives you more opportunities to pick up a good hand.

4. What else might happen?
   Other players may be eliminated before you have to post a blind.

The Skill of the Negotiators

1. What do many finalists do?
   They have a tendency to over value a large stack in relation to a small stack.

2. What is important to some players?
   Winning the tournament.

3. What does this mean?
   If you let them have the trophy, you can often get a favorable settlement.

4. What should you never do?
   Give the impression that you are eager to chop.

Other Topics

Playing Short-Handed Poker

1. What is safe to assume?
   That a player who lacks experience at tournament poker will properly adjust for a short-handed table.

2. What is short-handed poker similar to?
   Being at a full table after several people have passed.

3. Why is stud an exception?
   The total amount of antes in the pot will not be as large as it is in an eight-handed game.

4. When playing hold 'em what must you do on the flop?
   Make a lot of calls.

5. Why do you do this?
   To stop someone from stealing too much.

6. What if you fold every time you don't have a pair, a draw, or overcards?
   You are not calling enough.

7. What if you are playing stud?
   Follow similar advice.

8. What else should you keep in mind?
   A player's stack size will frequently dictate how he will play a marginal hand.

9. What if a player is anxious to chop?
   He will probably be playing conservatively.

10. What question should you ask yourself about your opponent?
    How did he get involved in this hand?

11. What if he was forced in?
    He is probably weak.

12. What if he has a comfortable stack and played of his own volition?
    Proceed with caution and give him credit for a good hand.

13. What if your adversary is a solid tournament player who knows to take advantage of tight play?
    You must be prepared to call him frequently.

14. What else should you be watching?
    The clock.

15. Why?
    The timing of the next increase in betting limits is sometimes more important than the skill of the players.

The Collusion Stage

1. What is sometimes correct strategy late in a tournament?
   Minimizing another player's chances of surviving rather than maximizing your chances of winning a hand.

2. If you have a strong drawing hand late in a tournament, what are the three situations when it is wise to raise even though the raise might help another player survive?

A. The player who you might be helping to survive will probably not pose an immediate threat even if he wins the hand.

B. There is a possibility that you might be able to eliminate more than one player.

C. There is a good possibility that you might be able to win a sizable pot.

3. When would you consider following the above recommendation for raising?

When you have a large stack.

4. What if you have a small or medium stack?

You should be primarily concerned with eliminating another player.

Stepping Up

No Rebuy Tournaments

Limit Games

1. How does opening action in a major tournament compare to a small tournament?
   It is usually more conservative.

2. Why is this the case?
   Opening limits are relatively large in relation to the size of the initial stack.

The First Three Levels

1. Describe the four types of players you will be against.
   The experienced and technically sound who can be expected to start off conservatively; the experienced and technically sound who can be expected to start off fast; the weak players; and the Kamikazes.

2. What will the majority of players be?
   The experienced and technically sound who can be expected to start off conservatively.

3. In the early going, what should you do if you have an opportunity to build your own stack?
   Go ahead and gamble.

4. What if you are seen as an inexperienced tournament player?
   Some of your opponents may try to intimidate you.

5. How do players in a major tournament compare to the average player in a small-stakes tournament?
They tend to be more predictable.

The Fourth, Fifth, and Sixth Levels

1. Should you go into survival mode?
No, it is too early.

2. What if you feel you have the upper hand?
Aggressively press your advantage.

The End Game

1. When does the end game usually begin?
During the seventh or eight level.

2. What effect does the size of the tournament pool have on strategy?
It has little bearing on strategy.

No-Limit and Pot-Limit Games

1. What is early action like?
It is extremely slow.

2. Who is favored in major no-limit tournaments.
Players with real poker skill as opposed to tournament skill.

3. Why is this the case?
The initial stack is larger relative to the starting blinds, the blinds are increased more slowly, and the edge that a good no-limit player has over the bad player is greater than it is in limit.

Constant Stack Rebuy Tournaments

Limit Games

1. At the beginning of the tournament, what is useful to know?
   Which players at your table are planning to make a rebuy and which are not.

2. What does this usually tell you?
   As a rule, players who plan to rebuy will be playing more aggressively than players who do not plan to rebuy.

3. What should you assume about the professionals at your table?
   That they will rebuy.

4. What else should you be doing?
   Paying close attention to the type of hands that players at your table are playing.

5. Why?
   Since there will be three or four rounds at the first betting limit, it should be possible to get a good read at your table.

The Rebuy Period

1. Why is playing fast a good strategy?
   It will maximize your chances of building a stack while leaving you the rebuy option.

2. What if you can't rebuy?
   You will be at a disadvantage to those who do rebuy, and should probably not play the tournament.

3. But what if you enter and can't rebuy?
   Still play aggressively.

4. Why?
   Your long-term prospects should be maximized.

The Intermediate Stage

1. What usually happens when the rebuy period ends?
   The pace of the action usually slows.

2. What should you do?
   Take advantage of tight play, and do not be afraid to try a steal if the opportunity presents itself.

3. What should you be watching?
   The clock and the position of the blinds.

Conclusion

As you can see, poker tournaments are very different from standard poker. There are many reasons for this, but the most important one is that the winner of the tournament does not collect all the money, even though he has won all the chips. This has many implications and impacts standard poker strategy in many ways. But most importantly, it means that you do not always have to try to maximize your expectation on virtually every hand as you would in a standard poker game.

Another characteristic of poker tournaments is that they play more like no-limit poker — even if the featured game is limit poker — than conventional poker. This is because players frequently go all-in early in a hand and there is "no play" on the later streets. This idea is more true late in a tournament and is one of the reasons why you need a good understanding of how hands perform "hot and cold."

Rebuy strategies figure into tournament play as well. In many events, correct rebuying will significantly impact your long-term results. Of course, in the short run anything can happen. But those of you who either don't rebuy, or rebuy improperly, will be at a distinct disadvantage to those expert tournament players who perform well in this area.

Finally, I want to again mention that there are very few players who can consider themselves experts at both tournaments and side games. While I do recognize that it is difficult to master both areas, I also believe that it not only can be done, but that there are a small number of people who have done it.

This brings to mind one last thought. Another tournament book out there talks about how you have to have some "flair" to be successful at poker tournaments. I don't buy this at all. In my opinion, what you need are knowledge and experience. Once you have acquired these attributes the flair should take care of itself.

180 Conclusion

Hopefully, this text will help to provide the knowledge. Now it is up to you to get the experience.

Appendix A
Glossary

Like any other avocation, the world of poker is full of colorful, sometimes ambiguous words and expressions. Following is a listing of a few of the more common poker expressions that are relevant to tournament poker.

Added money tournament: A tournament for which the sponsor contributes additional money to the tournament pool.

Aggressive player: A player whose style of play means that he is more likely to be betting or raising than calling.

All-in: Having all one's money in the pot.

Backdoor: To complete a hand unexpectedly while trying to make a different hand. For example, if a player had two pair and was hoping to make a full house but he unexpectedly makes a straight, he is said to have "backdoored" a straight.

Bad beat: To lose a pot in spite of having an exceptionally strong hand. Also, to lose a pot because a rival made a miraculous draw.

Bet blind: To bet before seeing the next card.

Bet for value: To bet a hand whose chances of winning are in doubt. It is nevertheless thought to be the best hand the majority of time your opponent calls.

Bicycle: Ace, 2, 3, 4, and 5 — the best possible hand in most lowball games. Also called a **wheel**. The term is used in all games.

Blind: In hold 'em, draw, and lowball, and some other games, a forced bet that one or more players must make to start the action on the first round of betting. The blind rotates around the table with each new deal. The person whose turn it is to bet is said to be in the blind.

Brick: A card that does not help. Also called a **rag** or a **blank**.

Bring-in: In stud games, a forced opening bet that is based on the first exposed card that players receive. In high and high-low split games, the player with the lowest ranking card is required to make the bring-in bet. For lowball stud (also called razz), the player with the highest ranking card is required to make the bring-in. "Bring-in" is also sometimes used as a verb. In such cases, it is synonymous with "bet." Also known as a **forced entry bet**.

Bully: To intimidate other players with aggressive play.

Buy-in: The cost of entering a tournament. For some tournaments, the entire amount goes into the tournament pool. For other tournaments, a nominal fee is deducted in order to help defray the cost of conducting the tournament. At an open table, the buy-in is the minimum amount of money required to sit down in a particular game.

Check: To decline to bet when it is your turn to act.

Check blind: To check a hand before seeing the next card (or cards).

Chip exchange: The process of exchanging small denomination chips for larger denomination chips when the smaller denominations are being withdrawn from a tournament. Chip exchanges are discussed in Part Seven.

Chop: An agreement among players to divide the money remaining in the tournament pool.

Come hand: A hand that has not yet been made with more cards still to be dealt. Thus, a four-card flush would be a come hand.

Counterfeit: In Omaha or hold 'em high-low split, a card that comes on board that numerically duplicates a card that is already in your hand and thus hurts your chances of winning low, and does you no good, but probably helps others.

Dealer button: A marker that is used to designate the player who will serve as the dealer.

Dog: Underdog. Not the favorite to win.

Entry fee: For poker tournaments, synonymous with **buy-in.**

Flop: In hold 'em and Omaha games, the first three exposed community cards, which are dealt simultaneously. The word is also used as a verb. For example, to flop a "set" is to make three-of-a-kind on the flop.

Fold: To drop out of a pot rather than call a bet or raise.

Freeroll tournament: A tournament for which there is no cost to enter the tournament.

Freezeout tournament: A tournament that is scheduled to continue until one of the players has won all of the chips. The overwhelming majority of poker tournaments are freeze outs. However, in practice, most tournaments end when the last few players agree to a split of the money remaining in the tournament pool.

Get quartered: To win only one-fourth of the pot in a high-low split game of poker.

Get there: To succeed in making a hand.

Give action: To bet, raise, or call liberally.

Give protection: To raise a player who is all-in in order to discourage other potential callers.

Go on tilt: To get upset and play poorly as a result of being upset. Also called **steaming.**

Gut shot: A draw to an inside straight. Also called a **belly buster.**

Guaranteed tournament: A tournament for which an amount of money is guaranteed by the sponsor. The guarantee usually applies to the total amount of money in the tournament pool or the amount that will be paid to the winner of the tournament.

Heads-up: A situation where only two players remain to compete for the pot.

In-house tournament: A small-stakes tournament that is conducted primarily for the benefit of regular patrons of the casino. These tournaments are therefore usually advertised only within the casino.

Kamikaze: A player who consistently bets or raises with a hand that does not warrant such aggressive action. Also called a **maniac.**

Kicker: The second ranking card in the hand when the hand does not contain a pair. When the hand does contain a pair, the highest ranking unpaired card.

Limp in: To enter the pot by calling in a situation where a raise might be the norm. In lowball, this is also called **gypsying-in.**

Loose player: A player who is inclined to play weak hands that most players would fold. A loose player may or may not be an aggressive player.

Lowball: A variety of poker games in which the best low hand wins in the showdown.

Monster: An extremely strong hand.

Multiple rebuy tournament: A tournament in which more than one rebuy is permitted.

Nuts: The best possible hand at any given point in a pot.

On a rush: To be on a winning streak.

On the come: Playing a hand that has not yet been made. For instance, if you bet with four cards to a flush, you are betting "on the come."

Open table: A game in a casino at a table that is not part of a tournament. Also sometimes called an **open game,** a **side game,** or a **live game.**

Pat hand: In draw poker games, a complete hand before the draw. A pat flush would be a five-card flush before the draw.

Pay off: To call a bet or a raise when you don't think that you have the best hand. Usually a player will "pay off" because he suspects that his opponent is bluffing, or because the pot is so large in relation to the size of the bet that a call is made in spite of reservations.

Payoff point: The number of players who will share in the tournament pool.

Percentage call: A call that is made because the cost of the call is small in relation to the size of the pot.

Play down: To reduce the number of chips in a stack in order to qualify to make a rebuy.

Play fast: To liberally bet or raise on a promising hand in order to get maximum return should the hand win.

Pocket cards: In games other than draw games, the cards that are dealt face down to the player and therefore cannot be seen by other players at the table.

Position: The spot in the sequence of betting in which a player is located. A player in the first position would be the first person to act; a player in the last position would be the last person to act.

Prop player: A player who is employed by the casino to stand by and fill in at tables that are in danger of disbanding due to a shortage of players. When actually playing, prop players play with their own money. Therefore, a prop player could easily lose his entire salary for the day as well as some of his own personal funds.

Qualification tournament: A tournament that is limited to participants who qualify under established criteria. Qualification may be based on almost any criteria including sex, the number of hours played in the casino, previous tournaments won, etc.

Rake: An amount retained by a casino from each pot as its fee for running the game. Instead of taking a rake many casinos now charge each player a time based fee that is collected every thirty minutes. Also called a **house cut.** Tournaments, however, have no rake.

Read: To arrive at a tentative conclusion about a hand, a player, or a table based on such factors as knowledge of players, betting patterns, and other observed evidence.

Rebuy: To purchase additional chips during the course of a tournament. Rebuys are permitted only for a specific period of time and are usually permitted only if a player has less than a specified number of chips. A rebuy usually takes one of the following forms:

1. **Constant stack rebuy:** The cost of the rebuy and the number of chips received remains unchanged throughout the rebuy period. Constant stack rebuy tournaments are discussed in Part Three.

2. **Progressive stack rebuy:** The cost of the rebuy remains unchanged but the number of chips received increases as betting limits increase. There are, however, virtually endless variations in rebuy procedures for progressive stack rebuy tournaments. For some tournaments, the

rebuy stack does not actually increase but the cost of a rebuy declines and multiple simultaneous rebuys are permitted. For example, if the buy-in is $20 for the initial stack of $200 in tournament chips, the rebuy stack might remain at $200, but the cost of the rebuy might be set at $10. However, a player would be allowed to make two simultaneous rebuys and receive $400 in tournament chips for $20. For our purposes, a tournament is considered to be a progressive stack rebuy tournament if the average cost of a chip declines during the rebuy period. Progressive stack rebuy tournaments are discussed in Part One.

Rebuy point: The maximum number of chips that a player may have when buying additional chips.

River card: The seventh and last card that is dealt in Omaha, stud, and hold 'em games.

Rock: A derogatory term for a very conservative poker player.

Rough: In lowball, a lesser hand in a particular category. For example, a

would be considered a rough seven because of the presence of the 6♦.

Satellite tournament: A tournament that is designed to provide the winner with a seat in a larger tournament.

Set: Three cards of the same rank such as three kings or three queens. Also called **trips** and **triplets.**

Scoop: To win the entire pot in a high-low split game.

Semi-bluff: To bet with a hand that you do not think is the best hand but which has a reasonable chance of improving to the best hand.

Service charge: Funds deducted from the buy-in to help offset the cost of conducting the tournament. Also called a **service fee** or **registration fee.**

Shootout tournament: A tournament in which play at the first table continues until one player has won all of the chips at the table. The winner at each table then advances to the second round of the tournament. Shootout tournaments are discussed in Part Five.

Short table: A table at which the number of players is less than the normal complement for the game that is being played. For example, since lowball is normally played with eight players, a short table would be a table at which less than eight players are seated.

Slowplay: To check or just call an opponent's bet with a big hand in order to win more money on later rounds.

Smooth: Opposite of a rough hand. For example, a

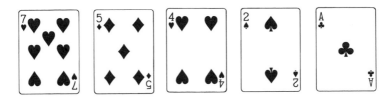

would be considered a smooth seven because no six is present.

Soft play: To avoid betting or raising with the winning hand as a favor to a friend.

Stack: The chips in a player's possession.

String raise: A raise whereby a player puts some chips in the pot without announcing his intention to raise, then returns to his stack in order to complete the raise. String raises are illegal in most casinos because they are thought to be an unethical attempt to test an opponent's reaction to a potential raise, before actually committing to make the raise.

Steam raise: A raise by a player who has raised, not because he has a strong hand, but because he is emotionally upset.

Sudden Sayonara Tournament: A tournament that ends when the number of players declines to a predetermined number. Sudden Sayonara Tournaments are discussed in Part Four.

Suited connectors: Cards that are of the same suit and adjacent rank. For example:

Super satellite: A multi-table satellite that is designed to provide entry (or entries) into major tournaments that have a relatively large buy-in.

Tell: A mannerism a player exhibits that may give away his hand.

Tight player: A very conservative player. A **rock.**

Tournament field: The total number of players who entered a tournament.

Tournament payout: The method used to determine amounts that will be paid to players who will share in the tournament pool. This usually takes one of the following forms:

1. **Percentage payback:** Amounts to be paid to final players are determined in advance as a percentage of the tournament pool. The overwhelming majority of poker tournaments are percentage payback tournaments.

2. **Chip count payback:** Amounts to be paid to final players are based on a percentage of the total chips that each player has after the last hand has been played. In other words, if after the last hand, a player had 95 percent of the tournament chips, he will receive 95 percent of the money that is in the tournament pool.

Tournament pool: The total amount of money that will be distributed to players who will share in the tournament prize money.

Tournament tie-breakers: The process of determining tournament placings when two or more players are eliminated during the playing of a hand. Tournament tie-breakers are discussed in Part Seven.

Turn Card: The fourth community card in hold 'em and Omaha games.

Wheel: Same as a **bicycle.**

World Series of Poker: An annual series of some fifteen poker tournaments with buy-ins ranging up to $10,000, which is held each spring at the Horseshoe Casino in Las Vegas. The competition is generally recognized as the premier competition among the best poker players in the world.

Appendix B
Recommended Reading

There are many books written on poker. These listed below are the poker books I like best and should be most helpful to your game.

1. *Caro's Book of Poker Tells* by Mike Caro (2003: Cardoza Publishing).

2. *Championship Satellite Strategy* by Tom McEvoy and Brad Dougherty (2003: Cardsmith Publishing)

3. *Fundamentals of Poker* by Mason Malmuth and Lynne Loomis (1992: Two Plus Two Publishing LLC).

4. *Gambling Theory and Other Topics* by Mason Malmuth (1994: Two Plus Two Publishing LLC).

5. *Getting the Best of It* by David Sklansky (1997: Two Plus Two Publishing LLC).

6. *High-Low Split Poker, Seven-Card Stud, and Omaha Eight-or-Better for Advanced Players* by Ray Zee (1994: Two Plus Two Publishing LLC).

7. *Hold 'em Poker* by David Sklansky (1996: Two Plus Two Publishing LLC).

8. *Hold 'em Poker for Advanced Players* by David Sklansky and Mason Malmuth (1999: Two Plus Two Publishing LLC).

9. *Improve Your Poker* by Bob Ciaffone (1997: Self-published).

10. *Omaha Hold 'em Poker (The Action Game)* by Bob Ciaffone (1992: Self-published).

11. *Poker Essays* by Mason Malmuth (1996: Two Plus Two Publishing LLC).

12. *Poker Essays, Volume II* by Mason Malmuth (1996: Two Plus Two Publishing LLC).

13. *Poker Essays, Volume III* by Mason Malmuth (2001: Two Plus Two Publishing LLC).

14. *Poker, Gaming, & Life* by David Sklansky (1997: Two Plus Two Publishing).

15. *Pot-Limit and No-Limit Poker* by Stewart Reuben and Bob Ciaffone (1997: Self-published).

16. *Seven-Card Stud for Advanced Players* by David Sklansky, Mason Malmuth, and Ray Zee (1999: Two Plus Two Publishing LLC).

17. *Seven-Card Stud: The Complete Course in Winning at the Medium and Lower Limits* by Roy West (1996: Poker Plus Publications).

18. *Sklansky on Poker* by David Sklansky (1994: Two Plus Two Publishing LLC).

19. *Super System: A Course in Power Poker* by Doyle Brunson (1979: Cardoza Publishing).

20. *The Theory of Poker* by David Sklansky (1999: Two Plus Two Publishing LLC).

21. *Tournament Poker for Advanced Players* (2002: Two Plus Two publishing LLC)

22. *Winning Concepts in Draw and Lowball* by Mason Malmuth (1993: Two Plus Two Publishing LLC).

23. *Winning Poker Systems* by Norman Zadeh (1974: Wilshire Book Company).

Index

NOTES